Come On, Get Happy

365 ways to feel good Jonathon Lazear

Element
An Imprint of HarperCollins*Publishers*
77–85 Fulham Palace Road,
Hammersmith, London W6 8JB

The website address is: www.thorsonselement.com

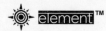

and *Element* are trademarks of
HarperCollins*Publishers* Limited

First published by Element 2004

1 3 5 7 9 10 8 6 4 2

© Jonathon Lazear

Jonathon Lazear asserts their moral right to
be identified as the author of this work.

A catalogue record for this book
is available from the British Library

ISBN 0 00717532 9

Printed and bound in Great Britain by
Clays Ltd, St Ives plc

This Book Is Dedicated To Four People
Who Always Make Me Happy:

Christi, Julie, Michael, and Ross

Acknowledgements

I'd like to sincerely and warmly thank my editor, Greg Brandenburgh, who actually came up with the concept of this book and patiently guided me through the process of writing it. He brought this to me at a particularly difficult time in my life, and the process of compiling these "happy ideas" became a positive therapeutic force for me, and I view that as an act of kindness.

My two associates, Christi Cardenas and Julie Mayo, were there for me, as they always are.

My friends Arlene and Harold Sheperd made my move back to New York nearly effortless, and their hospitality will long be remembered.

Jonathon Lazear
New York City
Autumn, 2003

Introduction

I hope that this little book of ideas and inspiration does, indeed, lead you and your loved ones to "get happy." In these stressful times it is, I believe, really necessary to indulge oneself in a little selfish pleasure. I think it is also important to acknowledge that doing something for another person—a partner, friend, co-worker, or even a stranger—is the kind of thing that gives us long-term happiness. Giving is the ultimate pleasure and I hope I have given you some ideas for self-satisfaction as well as concepts that will result in altruistic and non-self-involved ways to happiness. Remember, give until you smile and until it makes you and someone else happy—celebrate life's little pleasures, there is no need for extravagance, just creativity, humor, wit, kindness, and the surprise glow that inner happiness gives you.

In any case,

C'mon, Get Happy!

1

Come On, Get Happy

Take Inventory

Take stock in today. Are you happy? Have you been happier? If so, what were the circumstances of those happier times? Can you re-create any part or all of that time? It is common knowledge that, as an example, people who are approaching retirement feel that the best, happiest times are behind them, their life is essentially over.

Start planning for your freedom. You will continue to be productive, but now you will have the time to do what you want. Happiness will follow, once you know and believe that what is to come may exceed what came before.

"Good times can be replicated, at least in small ways. But living in the 'now' will bring you a measure of serenity."

Bertha Lewis Carpenter

2

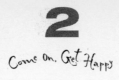

Come On, Get Happy

Daydream with an Atlas

One of my favorite things is to pan over the world atlas with my sons, who are interested in everywhere. We look at lakes and rivers that before were just names. We find wonderfully named towns and villages in the US (Shoulderblade, KY) and just imagine what Fiji must be like.

An atlas and an imagination are great partners, try it with your friends, loved ones, and kids.

"An ounce of imagination is worth a mile of parchment."

Anonymous

Visit a Nursing Home

Engage patients in real conversation. Listen to their stories.

Our older population sometimes seems to be forgotten, stored away in nursing homes and hives of "assisted living" apartments. They are alienated from society and thought to be hopeless, merely awaiting their final days.

There are, however, many seniors who long for conversation. They continue to have thoughts and feelings, convictions and beliefs, and also rich histories.

Make a habit of visiting these wonderfully interesting people. We have a lot to learn from them, all of us, so why not learn from someone who has "been there and done that."

"There is nothing stronger in the world than gentleness."

Han Suyin

4

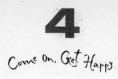

Come On, Get Happy

Tutor a Child

There are few things as important as giving.

Schools are everywhere and there are always children who need extra help. Helping a child to learn is like saving a life, and just how happy can that make any of us—it truly makes the world a better place to live.

"You cannot do a kindness too soon, for you never know how soon it will be too late."

Ralph Waldo Emerson

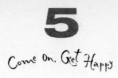

5

Come On, Get Happy

Reach Out to the Less Fortunate

Make sure your older, less fortunate, or handicapped neighbors have what they need. This will mean getting to know them, which should be a real bonus.

Does the elderly lady across the street have milk and eggs and enough heat? Perhaps a trip to the market would make her day, or a call to the gas company to make sure she is warm through the winter.

What about the wheelchair-bound war veteran next door? He might like to keep himself to himself, but sometimes he might like a companion, just someone to talk to about the day's news, or the weather.

Get to know your neighbors; we need each other for so many reasons.

"Character may be manufactured in the great moments, but it is made in the small ones."

Phyllis Brooks

Do Something Selfless . . . Just Because

Give something to the world, yes, the world. For example, become involved with an international organization that helps people in war-torn areas all over the world. These organizations are staffed by selfless, fearless professionals who provide much-needed help to other people, regardless of their nationality or politics. No matter how much or how little we earn in our work, we can all afford to send a little to help cover the costs of these amazing men and women.

Pick a charity you believe in. Giving anything to support a better world is better than doing nothing at all.

"Some people strengthen the society just by being the kind of people they are."

John W. Gardner

7

Come On, Get Happy

Create a Neighborhood Garden

Get people working together to create a place together that is for the common goal of growing your own vegetables or flowers, or both. "Community" will take on a new meaning as the garden grows and bears fruit.

Maybe it is an obvious thing to do, but not enough people would consider undertaking such a project. It is not just good, fresh tomatoes that you will harvest, it is the experience of creating something useful and healthy with a group of people you may never have met otherwise. You will find great commonalities between one another, and not just a love of sweet corn!

"We are more alike, than unalike."

Maya Angelou

8

Come On, Get Happy

Reading For Two

There are centers and organizations in many countries where you can record literature, fiction, and non-fiction as a service for the blind. Even if you don't have the facilities close to where you live, you can still read aloud to a blind person. It is a great gift—a dual gift—you get to learn and experience literature that you might not have otherwise chosen, and the blind will be given a gift that cannot be measured.

"Books may be the only magic."

Alice Hoffman

Get a Pet Cat

Cats are great, clean, fascinating animals. They, like all animals, each have a distinctive personality and you don't have to be an expert to realize it, just watch them play, fight, eat, and sleep. One cat can be a great friend, but two certainly doubles the fun and their interaction is ceaselessly interesting.

"Those who've never had the extreme good fortune of living with royalty, should just go out and get a cat."

Marjorie Benson White

10

Come On, Get Happy

Share Memories of Your Old Neighborhood

The old neighborhood—both my wife and I have shared the places where we grew up, went to school, and played schoolyard games with our sons. She gave us the town of Queens, New York—Forest Hills to be specific—and I, Columbus, Ohio, where we visited often during the holidays. It is amazing how interested and surprised your kids can be if you share your history with them—a guided tour of your yesterdays and all your favorite old haunts.

"If we don't know were we come from, how do we know who we are?"

Sr. Antoinette

Come On, Get Happy

Your Hands Aren't There to Sit on . . . Use Them!

Hobbies are great for all of us, at any age. They help us to broaden our world, meet people with similar interests, and can lead to a whole host of new experiences.

Stamp collecting, for example, can be fascinating. My oldest friend for years was devoted to his collection and, through him, I became interested too. Then came coin collecting, nothing highly valuable except what I learned from each piece and that was fun too.

"I shall affix the King's stamp upon this now, for it will stand the test of time and all men to come before it."

The Traitor by Justine Tewksberry

Go "Google" Someone

If you have lost track of an old friend, why not use your computer and "Google" them. Simply find the Google search engine, type in their entire name between quotation marks, and hit "search." If that doesn't trace them try adding what you believe to be their geographical hometown or state. It really does work. My wife tried last year, with some startling surprises.

"People take different roads seeking fulfillment and happiness. Just because they're not on your road doesn't mean they've gotten lost."

H. Jackson Brown Jr.

13

Look at the Moon

On the night of a full moon take blankets and your friends, kids, partner, or even go by yourself. Find a good spot to park everyone and just look up at the sky. Notice how the moon illuminates the landscape in unique ways—there is a reason why poets have talked of moonlight as being like no other kind of light.

We all live a hectic life, slowing down to notice the natural beauty that surrounds us is a gift that we can give to ourselves and to those we love.

"Shoot for the moon. Even if you miss, you'll land among the stars."

Les Brown

Join a Book Club

Book clubs are all the rage. There is such joy in finding a book and a writer who thrills you with his or her words, it is unlike any other discovery. Sharing your joy in a new book with your friends is a special gift to them, and to you.

I am one of those people who get so excited by the words of someone I have never read that I long to share what I have found and I cannot wait to read passages aloud.

"Books . . . the gift you never stop opening."

B. Dalton, Booksellers, advertising slogan

15

Come On, Get Happy

Make Popcorn

Nothing says "I'm in for the night, and I'm not coming out" like the smell of freshly made popcorn—you don't even have to have a new movie to watch. Popcorn is the one odor that is implicit, with a sense of safety and grounding, of home. It is nature's air freshener and the smell of comfort.

A number of times I've popped corn just for the ambience it affords. A realtor once told me that it is a great "homecoming" essence to have when you are trying to sell your home.

"My baby loves buttered popcorn . . ."

Buttered Popcorn by the Supremes

16

Come On, Get Happy

You Need a Six-Letter Word for "Happiness"

Are you good at crossword puzzles? I'm just OK at it. One of the "gold standard" crosswords is Will Shortz's *New York Times* Sunday crossword. They are always clever, usually way too clever for me, so actually finishing it, correctly, is a real accomplishment.

I have so enjoyed working on the puzzle on Sunday mornings with my wife and two sons. I come, in terms of ability, a distant fourth but I don't care, it is a great team effort and we always congratulate anyone who comes up with the answers to a particularly difficult word.

"Expand your vocabulary by 300% in just one week."

An old advertising slogan often seen on matchbook covers

17

Come On, Get Happy

Paint!

Get some good quality watercolor paper, some brushes, and a box of watercolor paints from your neighborhood art supply store. Go home and surprise your son, daughter, partner, best friend, whoever, with your work. Don't let anyone say, "I can't paint, I can't even draw!"

Painting is something that can make everyone happy. It is unexpected, it is a group activity, and it makes no difference if you have a lick of talent or not. It is the act of creativity, the use of tools and materials to turn out unique works of art.

"Painting is a nail to which I fasten my ideas."

Georges Braque

18

Come On, Get Happy

Run with the Bees

Don't be afraid to watch honeybees collect nectar and buzz around a field or your backyard, they are creating miracles. They are fascinating to watch: how one is drawn to clover, another to a rose. Watch them as they dart back and forth, knowing inherently exactly where to go and for how long.

Bees are not aggressive and do not sting unless threatened. Honeybees are here to make honey, if they were here to make pain there would be no honey. And honey is just one of the things that bees do in the grand choir that is Mother Nature's creation.

"It's the bee's knees."

1920s slang

Start Looking for Love in all the Right Places

Allow love and inspiration into your life. Look for possibilities, for people, for situations that will bring joy into your life. Don't keep a guard up and turn into a hermit. Don't let old unnecessary boundaries keep you emotionally locked away. Open up, and be patient.

"Just don't give up trying to do what you really want to do. Where there is love and inspiration, I don't think you can go wrong."

Ella Fitzgerald

20

Get Yourself Licked!

Buy or adopt a puppy either for yourself, for the family, or for your kids. The gift of a magnificent mutt goes a long way; they grow with you and will give years and years of pleasure. Every dog has its own distinct personality. Some are shy, some bold; all of them are sensitive and unique to themselves. A dog brings out the best in a person.

"Buy a pup and your money will buy love unflinching."

Rudyard Kipling

Give a Kid a Break!

The next time a kid bags your groceries and helps you to the car with them, engage him or her in conversation. Show them that you don't think what they do is demeaning; treat them as an equal. I see so many people just walk out there in silence, pop the trunk, and never exchange a word or a glance.

It is so easy to treat people as you would like to be treated yourself. It humanizes us and brings us closer to "what we can be." Just asking, "How is it going at school?" or "Did you go to the game last night?" can make two strangers feel a little closer.

"Make Someone Happy."

Song title popularized by Barbara Streisand

Expect the Unexpected!

I remember, vividly when my wife and I moved to Minnesota with our sixteen-month-old son, at the beginning of a whopper of a Minnesota winter. Minneapolis was exciting but what a change from New York City!

While the three of us huddled by a waning fire, along came George—a wonderful new friend with two of his kids. All three of them carried "first aid"—one son had an armload of wood for the fire, one had a bottle of wine, and the third a wonderful casserole for an electricity deprived house. How welcoming these things were.

"Miracles come in threes."

Katherine Crumrine

23

Come On, Get Happy

The Gang's All Here

Family reunions can be such fun; catching up with cousins you haven't seen in years and even meeting "new members" of the family for the first time. Bringing generations together for a day or a whole weekend can be magical for everyone. It gives us an opportunity, not only to find out about our aunts and uncles, but it also tells us, if we're willing to listen, a lot about ourselves.

Some advice—start planning as early as possible especially if family members are sprinkled all over the country, or even the world. It will all be worth it when they arrive.

"If you don't believe in ghosts you've never been to a family reunion."

Ashleigh Brilliant

Get All Wet

Get a pan big enough for two feet (your own), and fill it with water and Epsom salts or your favorite bubbles. Place it in front of the television or stereo, bring a chair and a towel, and soak away!

Your feet deserve a break today so come on, get your toes happy!

"Feet, don't fail me now . . ."

Anonymous

25

Come On, Get Happy

Swing!

Get yourself a hammock, string it on your porch or between two trees and use it!

It is such a simple thing; not expensive but so inviting, even to look at. Swaying in it on a sunny spring day, good book in hand, can be truly "mind cleansing." Don't think of it as selfish, think of it as a cradle for a weary soul.

Let the breeze carry you, and let your imagination take you away. Swing your way to a clear head and an open heart. Just being outdoors is sometimes a gift to yourself.

"Climb in and dream."

Come On, Get Happy

Remember a Treasured Memory

I remember, as a young kid, the joy I felt when my father and I would string the outdoor Christmas lights across our front porch, interweaving them in the wrought iron rails that were popular at the time.

It isn't always the "big things" that can take you back in time, and give you a warm glow. In fact, it's often those fleeting moments, a smile remembered, a meal shared, or a task finished in cooperation with another.

"I don't know what happens during the time these lights are in storage, but you can be sure that when it's time to put them back up, two or three bulbs have burned out."

"What Did You Do today, Daddy?"

The idea of taking your daughter or son to work is, I think, terrific. Most of the time our kids don't have any idea about what we do or where we do it, we just disappear for eight or ten hours a day and only occasionally do they hear us talking to our partner about our work.

You don't have to wait for the formal "take your son or daughter to work" day. Invite them to see you at your workplace or perhaps to a special occasion, maybe an employee birthday. In any case, sharing your work day world with your kids is important, not to instill a work ethic, just to see Mom and Dad in their place of business.

"Ignorance is not bliss, it's oblivion."

Phillip Wylie

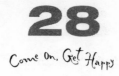

" . . . and . . . Action!"

My wife once had a great idea that turned into an unforgettable experience. Our son, Mike, was assigned a Shakespeare play to read at school and was dreading it. My wife, therefore, decided that both boys should join her in the backyard and they would each act out the various parts.

Not only did Mike instantly take to *Romeo and Juliet* but acting out the various parts gave him an additional interest: acting!

"The thing about performance, even if it's only an illusion, is that it is a celebration of the fact that we do contain within ourselves infinite possibilities."

Daniel Day Lewis

Come On, Get Happy

Stop Spending the Future

Instead of blindly using your credit cards, start using your debit card. It really is the same thing as cash, each time you use it cash is subtracted from your checking or savings account. This is a good way to learn how not to overspend.

Staying out of debt is, of course, a good thing and certainly something that will ease your mind and make you happy.

"A good debt is not as good as no debt."

Chinese proverb

Don't Try This at Work...

Go barefoot all day. Wear the most comfortable clothes you have—if it's a curtain, just remember to remove the rod! Don't comb your hair let yourself go, just for the day. I'm a firm believer in letting your hair down as often as you can get away with it. Pick a day, put it on the calendar, and look forward to a day by yourself, for yourself.

"The body never lies."

Martha Graham

Start Reading Some Wonderful Poetry

Pick what you want. An anthology is a wonderful source for poetry throughout the ages. Just page through it, savor your favorites, it may even lead you to write some of your own. I believe there is a poet in all of us, we just need inspiration and a safe, dry place to compose.

How many times have you said, or heard, "I can't draw," or the equivalent, "I can't write." I have never believed in this, it is just that most of us don't "practice" this kind of creativity. Many of us sadly view such activities, reading poetry, writing poetry, or drawing, as a waste of time.

"There is no frigate like a book to take us lands away. Nor any courses like a page of prancing poetry."

Emily Dickinson

Donuts All Round!

Do you work in a space with others? Why not, once in a while, say "coffee and donuts on me today?" It is a small gesture that will bring a smile to your co-workers' faces, and one to yours as well.

Sometimes it is the simplest things that can make you happy. No grand gestures are needed, just some thoughtfulness.

"Generosity lies less in giving much than in giving at the right moment."

Jean de la Bruyère

33

Come On, Get Happy

Just Smile, OK?

In a gloomy mood? Nothing on the near horizon to look forward to? Then try this: "Act as if . . ." the slogan that people in recovery use. It means act as though things are as you want them, keep positive, act positive, brighten up, act as if things are good and looking up for you.

Sometimes you have to do some positive self-talk. It can change your attitude and turn a bad day around. Take a look at all the good in your life, there has got to be many things to be grateful for.

"Smile and feel ten years younger; worry and get gray hair."

A Chinese proverb

34

Come On, Get Happy

Go Back to School

No, I don't mean re-enrol. I am assuming, like most of us, you had at least one teacher who stood out, who was an inspiration and taught you things you thought you would never learn. Go back and visit him or her. If you haven't already, tell them how much you valued your time in the classroom with them.

We sometimes forget those who were important to us "way back when." I had a brilliant high-school English teacher. He infused his teaching with a true and unmistakable passion for poetry and to this day I find a great deal of comfort in reading poetry, this is because of him.

"A teacher affects eternity, he can never tell where his influence stops."

Henry Brook Adams

35

Hands-On Happiness

Trade a shoulder and back massage with a friend or partner. It takes so little time, even in the middle of a busy day, but it will be a stress relief for both of you. Human touch means a great deal. It has been proven that people who do not have human contact are prone to depression, impatience, and don't heal from illness as quickly as those that allow the intimacy and kindness of "touch."

You have probably seen those books, kiosks, or small salons in populated places like shopping malls and airports that offer "twenty minute stress busters"—shoulder and neck massage between planes or stores, why not?

"A stranger's hands—once thought to be anathema, will warm your heart and tender your soul."

Beatrice Vincent

Come On, Get Happy

Rent or Buy a Funny Video

Although many of the current comedians are brilliant, creative, and have some pretty amazing ways of looking at the world, try going to your video rental store and checking out some of the older classic comics. Try *George Burns and Gracie Allen*, *I Love Lucy*, *The Sid Ceaser Show*, *Milton Berle's Texaco Theater*, and *Erne Kovak*, to name just a few. The classics will crack you up and you will see who influenced many of today's best comedians.

**"Laughter shall drown the raucous shout;
And, though these shelt'ring walls are thin,
May they be strong to keep hate out and hold love in."**

Louis Untermeyer

37

Come On, Get Happy

Don't Forget Your Dreams

Keep a dream journal. If you are lucky, like me, you dream a lot and remember all or part of them but you know how you quickly forget them again. To stop this from happening, one of my sons bought me a dream journal to record my dreams in.

In my family, we take great joy in telling one another our dreams over breakfast. Some are funny, some just puzzling, but it is an act of exchange and wonderment that keeps us close.

"Dreaming permits each and everyone of us to be quietly and safely insane every night of our lives."

Charles Fisher

Just for the Fun of it

Baby-sit for nothing. Give someone you care about some time away from their kids and you can enjoy yourself with them, especially if you don't have any of your own. Get down on the floor with them, run around the house, make cookies, give everyone a treat, and yourself one as well.

If you love kids, and feel like one yourself some days, give yourself a lift and act like one. Spring the parents and have a heck of a good time.

"How do they do it? Parents I mean, especially with three kids and two jobs. I'm exhausted from one weekend."

Anonymous

39

Come On, Get Happy

Wrap it up

Wrap your gifts in the most imaginative way you can. If the recipient is a car lover, buy an old car manual and use several pages as wrap. If you are giving someone a DVD of his or her favorite movie, why not wrap it up in the movie listings from a newspaper. A joke book, the comic page, of course.

When you allow yourself to get creative and try new ideas, it is a gift you give to yourself. Have some fun with something that would normally seem mundane.

"Come on, get creative."

Take the Long Way Home

Take the back roads and ignore the fast lane. Fill your tank, take a look at a map, but ultimately follow your own road. Why must we always get to our destination at breakneck speed? The joy of taking "the road not taken" is finding forgotten towns, and it may even lead you to take in the day in a new and simple way.

Last summer, my son and I took some back-road weekend trips with no real destinations in mind. We came across a whole range of surprises that lead us into great conversation.

"Travel can be one of the most rewarding forms of introspection."

Lawrence Durrell

Lose Yourself in a Bookstore

Lucky me, I stayed in Chicago a day after my work was done and spent the day hunting out the best used bookstores in town and browsing every stack of books I could. I left my watch in my hotel room as my stomach always knows what time it is. Of course, any big city has good bookstores, new and used, but where else but Chicago can you find some great out-of-print treasures, and get the best pizza in America?

"Find out what's splendid about a place, a town, a region, and indulge yourself in the best they have to offer."

Campbell Sinclair

Take Your Community Education Brochure Seriously

Almost every community, large and small, has a learning center—a place where you can learn new things, or old things new ways.

Try a ceramics class or learn to bake bread. Take a look and find out what strikes your fancy—perhaps it will be growing Bonsai trees, whatever your pleasure.

"Intellectual growth should commence at birth and cease only at death."

Albert Einstein

43

Get Crazy

Ever wanted to jump into the pool with all of your clothes on? Most people have, and time is wasting so do it, do it sober, but do it. You don't even have to wait for a wild party, just make sure your keys, wallet, and non-waterproof watch are safely ashore and jump in after a really stressful day.

"Twenty years from now you will be more disappointed by the things that you didn't do than by the ones you did do."

Mark Twain

44

A Kodak Moment

Ever since my boys were born, we have always made a conscious effort to have film in one of our cameras, for those camera-ready moments when you know they will debut at something. Our most treasured photos are those that were not "posed," but were taken at moments that otherwise would had to have been trusted to memory.

A whole range of emotions flood back when you come across one of those impromptu snapshots, they really are the best.

"Don't leave home without it."

American Express advertising slogan

Make a Date . . . and Keep it

Once a week, regardless, go out on a date with your spouse. You don't have to go to a four-star restaurant and spend a fortune, although once in a while that is a real treat. Maybe take in a movie, go for a long walk and a talk, a bike ride, a glass of wine at a favorite bistro. Do both of you a favor and get away from it all.

Life is hectic, for most of us. The pressure from our careers, our kids, paying the bills; you name it, we all have a lot to cope with. So give yourself the pleasure and freedom of just "you two time."

"You don't love a woman because she is beautiful, she is beautiful because you love her."

Anonymous

46

Come On, Get Happy

Start Collecting

So many of us think that collecting original artwork—paintings, drawings, etchings, even sculpture—is beyond our means financially, or even intellectually, but this is not the case. In some cities and towns, many communities have street fairs that include art of all kinds. Some of it will reveal itself to be more craft-oriented (not that there is anything wrong with that) but you will be able to find things that capture your imagination and something that will enhance your home and your life.

Take a chance and start collecting. So what if what you take home never increases in value, you will enjoy your choice for many years to come.

"Even Gertrude Stein took a chance on a guy named Picasso."

Take Yourself to the Movies

Going to the movies alone is not a lonely experience, especially if the movie is a good one. You can soak up the story and go with the plot and the characters all by yourself. While it is fun to discuss the movie afterwards, sometimes it is refreshing not to have to justify or rehash a film, especially if it wasn't that good.

Once the lights have gone down, who will know if you have a date or not? You are there to see a film, not necessarily to socialize, so have fun all by yourself.

"When the lights go down, it's just me and the screen."

Try That Extra Touch

Make yourself and someone else happy by going the extra distance. Always send a "thank you" note after a special gift or a dinner out with friends who paid for the evening, or just because someone was kind.

Sometimes simple acts of kindness, a soothing conversation, a quiet walk with a friend, or a surprise batch of photographs of loved-ones far away is a simple expression to say how you were touched by their generosity.

"Any kindness, no matter how small or how large a feeling, should elicit gratitude to those who accepted it."

Italian proverb

49

Come On, Get Happy

Improvise

Sometimes you just don't feel like shopping for food. You have come home, dog-tired from a day at work, thrown your coat on the sofa and the last thing you want to do is put it back on for a trip to the supermarket.

So this is what I have done in the past, it is fun and by its very nature, inventive. Try creating something from what is already in the pantry and refrigerator, experiment. Unless you have absolutely no food in the house you will have a good time being creative in the kitchen; my personal favorite has been cold, curried broccoli and bacon soup, honest!

"When in doubt, innovate."

The Splendid Table, Lynn Rosetto Kasper

Unplugged, Part 1

I have a friend who does not have the following, and never will:

- A phone answering machine
- Voicemail
- A fax machine
- A computer (no email)
- A television
- Call waiting
- A second line

This is what she does have:

- An award-winning garden
- The best-selling books that she wrote on her old typewriter
- A lot of good close friends
- An old Mercedes Benz
- An astonishingly brilliant sense of humor
- Great kindness

June is not weird, she is happy not to have the above clutter in her life to complicate it. She knows who she is, and doesn't need machines to define her.

"Making the simple complicated is commonplace—making the complicated simple, awesomely simple—that's creativity."

Charles Mingus

51

Take a Deep Breath

This is a great stress reliever, I use it daily and it really works: Take in a deep, deep breath and hold it, gradually and slowly let yourself exhale. You will feel almost instant relief. Do it again and you will feel the tension disappear from your neck and shoulders.

It clears my mind to practice this. Shallow breaths are a sign of stress. If you remember this little concept, I think you will adopt it in your daily life.

"Okay now, one, two, three take a deep cleansing breath . . ."

La Maze instructor for expectant mothers

52

Come On, Get Happy

Go on a News Diet

I'm on a news diet right now but at first I had real trouble resisting the twenty-four-hour news channels. I'm not saying that ignorance is bliss, I think most adults need to have an understanding of what is going on in the world, but too much bad news is just that, too much. Since the world is a dangerous place, and always has been, I don't need to be reminded three times a day.

Don't be the ostrich that buries its head in the sand but lighten up on your news intake, too much can bring you down all day.

"I do not like to get the news, because there has never been an era when so many things were going right for so many of the wrong persons."

Ogden Nash

Just Buy the Spray, Not the Car

Now, if you're a pure urbanite and take trains, planes, buses, but not automobiles, you probably won't get this: "The new car smell." I'm not kidding, I don't know what that unmistakable odor is composed of, but it brings joy to the new car owner and his or her passengers. No-one ever gets into a new car and doesn't say, "Oh, that new car smell."

The new car is a source of pride and the smell of it may wear off too quickly. Where I get my car washed, however, they actually spray the smell of new car inside as they dry it off, much cheaper than a new car!

"'New' doesn't equate with 'happy' or there wouldn't be any antique stores."

Wilfred Ford

Cool it

When you order ice cream in Europe you are given "multiple scoops." In America, you have to specify how many scoops you want and it is usually just one flavor. Next time you are itching for some ice cream, be European and order two or three scoops—treat yourself.

Life is too short to short-change yourself with "not quite enough" of one of the world's favorite desserts.

"Age doesn't seem to diminish the extreme disappointment of having a scoop of ice cream fall from the cone."

Jim Fiebig

Try the Soothing Sound Of Falling Water

Collect some rocks, foliate, gravel, and get your hose—you are going to build yourself a little fountain. It doesn't have to be a work of art, just arrange the rocks and let the water trickle down over them; use just enough water to make the fountain peacefully audible. The making of the fountain and the end result will be soothing in so many ways.

Water has such healing properties. Working with it, making a natural place for it, and allowing yourself to create with it will be a happy, magical experience.

"There is no way to peace. Peace is the way."

A.J. Muste

Here's the Wheel . . . I'm on Vacation

Now that my kids are licensed (and very good) drivers, it is a treat for me not to have to drive everywhere. I see things, in what should have been familiar terrain, for the first time! I never noticed the house that was tucked behind that hedge or that a new bank seemed to have been built overnight.

Being a passenger rather than a chauffeur is a treat, now it is my turn to look out of the side windows.

"Daddy, teach me to drive."

My sons at age ten

Look for Something You Aren't Looking For

Go to an antique or second-hand store, they are places that are always intriguing and you never know what you will find. One of my sons collects old license plates so I always see if I can add to his collection. I also enjoy buying old *Life*, *Look*, *The New Yorker*, or *Time* magazines. It is fun to look back, sometimes just a few years but I always try to look for issues that were published during my parents' lives and around the time when my children were born, as well as magazines with historical significance.

"Sometimes going back is going forward."

Sarah Bernstein

58

Leave Your Watch at Home

I understand not everyone can do this but do try, or at least think about it—take your watch off and leave it off. Start the weekend and see how it feels. Do you really need to know what time it is every second? (In some careers you do but in most you don't.) I find the feeling freeing and I feel less compulsive when I don't know "exactly" what time it is.

We can become slaves to time, don't let it happen. Everyone has the same twenty-four hours in a day so stop running. Stop looking at your wrist to make sure you are gaining an extra minute here, a minute there.

"Oh, how freeing it was to stop looking at my watch like it was going to explode or something."

Cook up Some Comfort

They call it comfort food and the connotation is that it is a dish that your mother made when you were a kid—burger and cheese, chicken soup, vanilla pudding, all of the above? What is preventing you from cooking the same food now? Why not? Because television and general food trends (which are also interesting and fun) tell us that if there is no balsamic vinegar or olive oil in the house the food police fine you?

What happened to fish sticks, chocolate milk, mashed potatoes? Why not indulge yourself, cook up a batch of whatever your comfort food is, and curl up with a good film.

"Food is an important part of a balanced diet."

Fran Lebowitz

Climb on and Start Peddling

Have you ridden a tandem bicycle? You know that old song, "A bicycle built for two?" Well, you can rent the real thing, and within a few minutes it can turn into a wonderful afternoon with a friend, wife, husband, or just about anybody. Don't forget the picnic basket, find a place at your favorite park and make the whole experience complete.

"The journey is the reward."

Taoist saying

61

Luxuriate in Bed

Indulge completely. Buy good quality sheets and pillowcases. Invest in what we do eight hours a day; I believe we sleep better when we are surrounded by a little luxury and absolute comfort. Just don't bring the crackers to bed with you, it may reverse the effect of fine Egyptian cotton.

Who says you have to scrimp when it comes to your bedroom linens? It is a place of refuge and rest. Do yourself a great favor and splurge on you and your partner.

"One of the most adventurous things for us to do is to go to bed. For no one can lay a hand on our dreams."

E.V. Lucas

62
Come On, Get Happy

You Don't Have to Go to Maui

You don't have to go to Hawaii to make, or receive, a real flower lei—the wonderful, fragrant orchid necklace that greets you in Hawaii. A great way to "smell the roses" is by wearing them.

With a little strand of florist's wire and a handful of orchids, you can practically hear the waves crash on your lawn at home. Take the trip . . .

"If I had but two loaves of bread, I would sell one and buy hyacinths, for they would feed my soul."

The Koran

63

Come On, Get Happy

Scare Yourself Happy

Do you like horror movies? With all the money involved in making scary films, we must like to get frightened, so take yourself and a friend out for some fun and fright.

Friday the Thirteenth, I Know You're in There, I Know What You Did Last Summer, and classics like *Dial M For Murder,* and *Psycho*—rent some screams of delight.

"The suspense is terrible . . . I hope it will last."

Oscar Wilde

64

Make a List

Make a list of just five books you wish that you had read then, go to the library or your favorite bookstore and get the first one on the list, if you buy all five at once, you may be overwhelmed. Pace yourself, and don't "over-promise" yourself, it is supposed to make you happy from the brain down and to be an enjoyable gift to yourself.

I missed so many of the "classics"—that's where I'm starting . . .

"When a new book is published, read an old one."

Samuel Rogers

65

Go for a Night Swim

Have you ever gone for a night swim? My son told me how much he and his friends love to go out in the lake on a hot night and just float on the waves.

Most of us would just enjoy watching the moon's reflection on the surface of the water, but try a dip in the lake to cool off and get happy.

"Dad, we just floated, and looked up at the stars. It was so quiet, and we all had a good talk. It was awesome."

Ross Lazear

Pick up Where You Left off

Did you take three years of French, Spanish, or some other foreign language in school? Have you forgotten most of what you learned? Why not buy some language tapes, or sign up for adult language classes at a nearby university, and become fluent in that language all over again.

You may do this in preparation for a visit to Spain, South America, or Paris. Be prepared, and have fun re-acquainting yourself with a language that will enrich your life and travels.

"England and America are two countries separated by the same language."

George Bernard Shaw

Sign up Today

Join a local theater company. You don't have to be an actor, dancer, singer, or performer of any kind, there are so many other things to do—props, creating and building sets, lighting, costumes, make-up. The point is that "theater people" are an interesting lot. The theater brings together a vast variety of people—most of them with great backgrounds and interests. You will enjoy this new group of people—even if you are only painting scenery.

It is important to belong to a "community." You will find great new friends, enrich your life, and broaden your talents and interests at the same time.

"Acting is merely the art of keeping people from coughing."

Sir Ralph Richardson

Keep it Simple

Streamline your life. Must you accept every invitation you get? Does your lifestyle keep you out almost every night after work; are you constantly over-booked and over-burdened? Why burn out before dinner? Leave a block of time, each day, for doing something spontaneous.

Take a step back, and assess your calendar. Do you really need to make an appearance at every party, church function, town meeting, restaurant opening, and birthday party?

It may be time to simplify your life. Choose one or two of those "nights out" that are really important, and limit yourself to those evenings. Slowing down can save your life, both literally and figuratively. Being more of a "homebody" has its rewards.

"Next thing I'll do is cancel all of next week."

Anonymous

When in Doubt, Throw it out

I learned this one the hard way. For many years, I kept every Christmas card, every letter, every note the kids wrote—nothing missed my compulsion to try to hang onto the evaporated moment of first seeing and reading all of the mementos of my past.

Finally, some months after I moved into an apartment drastically smaller then the house I had just sold, I came to the realization that all the birthday cards and childhood drawings in storage were just that: in storage. What is past is past.

I feel much more free and forward thinking in my attitude now that I'm not lugging those memories around.

"Physical matter is not necessarily the tangible proof of love."

Simon Lindquist

A Job Done Well

If you take on any responsibility—at work, in your church, club, PTA—whatever it is, do it right. Don't slough it off; you and your conscience are on the line. Your self-image will be stronger knowing that you saw it through and did it your way.

Self-respect is so important. We can look for it externally, but we can also find it internally. Doing good by doing well is a phrase I like to think of often.

"There's a right way, my way, and your way."

Fletcher English

Listen to Others, Not Just Yourself

Oh, did I make a mistake. Seduced, or allowing myself to be seduced, I bought an SUV (Sports Utility Vehicle). I could not believe I had done it, my wife and friends all said, "Don't do it," or "Why do you want one of those?" Well I got one, it cannot pass a gas station, it is a luxury automobile so it needs attention and it has gadgets, lots of gadgets. I can't wait to go full circle and try one of those semi-electric/gas cars that can go about nine hundred miles on a gallon of whatever.

It is so freeing when you are not a slave to a car, or anything else for that matter. Status, or the search for status, is a dangerous thing. Think about what you really need in a car, not what someone tells you that you need. Happiness is getting to your destination safely, not regally.

"Habit is stronger than reason."

George Santayana

Dude, Where's My Horse?

Have you ever been horse riding? It can be a great vacation for the whole family, or perhaps just go by yourself. You don't have to be a super athlete to enjoy a week in the countryside on the back of a gentle horse. Just listen to the instructors, they are there to help the novice learn the ropes, I mean the harness.

"A horse! A horse! My kingdom for a horse."

William Shakespeare

Come on, Get Happy

Believe in Luck

If we believe in luck it gives us hope, and we all need hope. How many times a day do we think about hope and wish for luck? So what is the harm in having faith in luck?

We need to allow ourselves to dream about possibilities and what good things can come our way, sometimes by chance and sometimes by our own design.

"It's hard to detect good luck. It looks so much like something you've earned."

Frank A. Clark

Pick up a Copy Of 'The Anti-Martha'

Ever read the magazine *Real Simple*? At first I thought it was a sure-to-fail niche U.S. magazine. But then I began to read it more closely, my wife had ordered a subscription as I am a magazine fanatic, and found articles that really celebrated making life easier, and without question, more enjoyable.

I was wrong to pre-judge this magazine. Its cause is noble, without any pretension. It talks of unravelling complications that lead to life-clutter, things, and processes that get us bogged-down and make us unhappy.

"Keep it simple."

. . . as they say in A.A., they are right.

Call Ahead

If you are having an important lunch or dinner in a restaurant, and the tab is on you, whether it be with a friend, business partner, or potential client, call the restaurant before you arrive. Give them your credit card number and add a good tip to avoid any awkwardness when the check is delivered to your table.

There is something very elegant and hospitable about being able to say: "It is taken care of . . ."

" 'Check please' can end a great lunch on a sour note."

Expect the Best...

... and you may not be disappointed. I have long-term experience with being "the boss" and I like to think that my history bears out the theory that if you expect people to do their best, and you allow them to do so, they almost always come through for you.

I think this is true in nearly every kind of relationship, not just the employer/employee, so adjust your attitude and allow others to excel.

"Showing trust and openness usually creates trust and loyalty."

Caroline Nelson

77

Come On, Get Happy

Go to the Market

Go to your local farmers' market or greengrocer and create a basket of exotic fruits and vegetables. Don't just include tomatoes and cucumbers, what about some unusual squash, star fruit, mangos, kiwi, or melons. It will make a great house gift and you will have fun, not only choosing the food but deciding how to cook and prepare the goodies.

Today's mysterious fruit may turn into tomorrow's staple.

"Never eat more than you can lift."

Miss Piggy

Laugh out Loud

Someone told me that the act of laughing releases endorphins in the body. I am not going to try and find out if this is true or not, what would be the point? I want to think it is true, so I believe it.

I am big on laughter. I love good sitcoms, *Will and Grace*, *Friends*, *Saturday Night Live*, my friend and client Al Franken. Dammit, I love to laugh.

Even in the bleakest of times, laughter, as *The Readers' Digest* used to say, "is the best medicine." I agree, go where laughter is prevalent and expected.

"Nobody ever died of laughter."

May Beirbohm

One, Two, Three, Faster

Feeling a little out of shape? Do you have a friend who also needs to tighten up a bit? Why not get together before work and put yourselves through the paces? Exercise is always more pleasurable if you have a friend who is joining you in the battle of the bulge, and who can spot for you too.

It's not competitive, just supportive, and you can begin looking forward to it, as you become one another's "personal trainers."

"Use it or lose it."

Jimmy Connors

Unplugged, Part 2

Are you a slave to a ringing phone? I'm talking about your home phone. We all have to answer our phones at work, I think.

If you are in the middle of reading to your kids, putting them to bed, kissing your partner, making a great loaf of bread, or just making dinner, does the phone need to interrupt?

If you are expecting an emergency call from the hospital, regarding the health of a loved one, then that is a good reason to head for the phone. Otherwise, and especially at dinnertime, let it ring. In your heart and head you know what to "pick up."

"Let it go to voicemail."

A prevalent statement

Play Monopoly

Play Monopoly or any board game that you played as a kid. Do it with good friends, those who may be described as "adult" friends. It will bring back great memories, jokes, and a well-worn, warm feeling.

Have some old-fashioned fun, remember being a kid again—those old board games are as good now as they were "back then."

So, it's chocolate milk all around, let the kid come back again.

"Who said: 'You can't go home again'? He was wrong."

Linda Fredricks

Honor Thy Father and Mother

Have you lost a loved one? Perhaps a grandmother or grandfather, or even a dog or cat. I think it is a wonderful and happy job to plant some kind of a favorite flowering perennial by the gravesite. A flowering vine? A crawling rose? Tulips?

Some may find this morbid but the act of keeping something "alive" next to someone you have lost may make you happier and may help to keep their memory alive.

"I feel at peace at the stone; it is quiet, and we are alone."

Anonymous

83

Be Your Own Fashion Advisor

When I was younger, I would not stop buying clothes. The newest fashion, the newest and most "in" color; the newer, the better.

Talk about "keeping up with the Joneses" and what a way to waste money and time, all in the name of vanity. Now I have a solid selection of just a few things. They are not up-to-the-minute in terms of current trends or styles, but I'm happy not being a fashion victim anymore.

"Fashions fade—style is eternal."

Yves St Laurent

Take a Hike

Break a sweat, climb some hills, breathe hard, and take rests. Stop and listen to the birds, the wind, or water, take in the scenery. You don't have to drive for hundreds of miles to find a place to do some rugged climbing and walking; chances are, there are places fairly close by.

After an afternoon or early morning hike, you feel rejuvenated. It is exhilarating to be physical and to challenge yourself while taking in the outdoors. Make it a gift to yourself as often as you like.

"Placing one foot in front of the other—that is how we get to where we need to be."

A Native American proverb

85

Come On, Get Happy

Try This!

I really don't know anything about flower arranging, but I have always been intrigued by people who know how to make a seemingly disharmonious bunch of flowers into a an eye-popping masterpiece.

One day I stopped by my local flower shop and just watched the owner clip and shape, add and subtract flowers and greens until she had an absolute work of art in a vase. Maybe you could take a course?

"I perhaps owe having become a painter to flowers."

Claude Monet

Give 'em a Break

I live in a city where there are many, extraordinarily gifted musicians on street corners, in the subway, and in the parks. Many of these people are students, and many are amateurs who make the city a better, more vibrant, and more musical place to live.

If I have spare change, or a dollar, I always give them what I can. I support "street music," it makes all of us happier people.

"Extraordinary how potent cheap music is."

Noel Coward

Come On, Get Happy

Feed the Ducks

When my boys were little kids, we loved to go to the local pond or lake with a bag of bread to feed the ducks. The kids thought it was just about the greatest thing to do.

We then graduated to skipping rocks; funny how you can enjoy the lake without getting wet.

"Human beings were invented by water as a device for transporting itself from one place to another."

Tom Robbins

Buy the Greatest Hits

Who were your favorite music makers while you were growing up? Do you miss them and their music? Jefferson Airplane, Nat King Cole, Diana Ross and the Supremes, Frank Sinatra, Elvis? Go out and buy your favorite entertainers' "greatest hits." Why be embarrassed? If you loved the music then, maybe you will still tap your foot to the oldies.

"Baby, baby, where did our love go?" That was one of mine, I hear it on the radio (and on my stereo, when I'm in the mood), and BINGO! I'm back in 1964 remembering some of the good times that happened only once in the days when you are on the way to "adulthood."

"Come on, get happy."

Irving Berlin

Soar with Your Strengths

This is the title of a great book by Don Clifton and Paula Nelson. How many of us have been a square peg shoved into a round hole? If a job does not fit—like shoes that are too small—get rid of it. Try to quantify your strengths, find out what they are. There are some very good self-tests you can buy to discover what you are good at, and what you are not.

You don't always have to take a test to find out, at least in part, what you are good at or what you love doing but, as the old saying goes, *Do What You Love and the Money Will Follow* (this is also the title of another great book).

"I think knowing what you cannot do is more important than knowing what you can do."

Lucille Ball

Sleep Your Way to Better Health

Like many people, I have trouble, at least occasionally, in getting to sleep. Most of the time what keeps me awake is anxiety and thinking about a million things: "Oh, I should have done that," or "Oh, I forgot to call so-and-so." My mind starts to go into overtime.

A friend of mine told me he too had similar experiences. His doctor told him to think of one thing, a positive thing, and not to let other thoughts intrude. Immerse yourself in a good memory, or a positive goal you want to meet. It works for me, I get to sleep and have a deeper and less troubled sleep by using this method.

"Sleep, it cures everything."

Monica Brank

Pay it Forward

This is something guaranteed to make you happy—pay your credit card debt in full every month. If you can do this you will limit your use of the card as you automatically observe a budget and consequently don't feel burdened and anxious about over-spending. That plastic does not signify an endless credit line.

If you have ever been really stretched to make a credit card payment or habitually feel squeezed by your monthly payments, then you know that it does not make you happy. Try hard to be discerning about your use of "the card" and what you're buying with it. Do you really need it?

"The real measure of wealth is how much you'd be worth if you lost all your money."

Anonymous

Don't Overdo It

As a family, we learned this the "hard way." We used to spend a huge amount of money buying our kids Christmas gifts. We got into really enjoying finding all the "right things", the perfect gifts for each of the boys. Over time we pulled back, spent less, and tried to be creative about what we got for them. They ended up enjoying what we got for them more, especially because there wasn't so much "stuff."

It is so much more enjoyable to search out "special" gifts for people. Things they will really love and use for a long time, rather than just showering them with a million different gifts.

"Nothing in excess."

Anonymous

Be Content for a Change . . . Another Word for Happy

"Happiness" and "contentment" are not at opposite sides of any spectrum. Sometimes we may get a little carried away with the notion of "glee," or extreme happiness but many of us also find joy in a quieter way, what one may call "contentment."

You can't hit a home run every time. Many of us are pretty competitive, and think we have to hit one hundred every time we are given a test, but you can't always be perfect and anyway, who is keeping score? Give yourself some breathing room, some space to be the best you can without being perfect.

Perfectionism is a terrible problem for those who are saddled with it. Being "perfect" is mythical, and leads to crushed hopes and certain failures. Try hard not to get into that rut.

"The world is full of people looking for spectacular happiness while they snub contentment."

Doug Larson

Meet the Neighbors

Recently, after a move back to New York City, I have tried to get to know my neighbors, at least to some degree. I have lived in big cities all my life and know that it is easy to become invisible to those who live across the hall or across the street from you. You don't have to be anyone's best friend, but knowing neighbors can bring you some sense of happiness and serenity.

Science has proved that one's wellbeing is enhanced by the act of smiling. Why not add a "hello" to that smile, when you see your neighbor?

"To a friend's house, the road is never long."

Danish proverb

Throw Open the Windows

This idea depends on where you live in the world, and what time of the year you are reading this. On the next sunny, warm day, open up all your windows and let the fresh air roam throughout your house or apartment—"un-stuff" it. Get some fresh air circulating in every room. Even if you can do it only once in a while, it is a great way to clear the "overused" oxygen that has been hanging around the house too long.

I, personally, love the smell in the air after a good, soaking rain. After a downpour, I love to open up the house, and let that wonderful natural odor come into every corner of every room.

"Walking in the rain with the one you love . . ."

Neil Sedaka

Look in the Mirror and Grin

I have a little sign taped to my bathroom mirror, an old friend gave it to me and it says: "Good morning, handsome." Of course it is false advertising but it was a sweet gesture and conjures up thoughts of the friend who made it. I like to think of myself as OK looking, perhaps even handsome when I'm dressed up, but who looks great with "bed-head" and a in wrinkled T-shirt? Brad Pitt, probably.

"Better keep yourself clean and bright; you are the window through which you must see the world."

George Bernard Shaw

Give Yourself the Animal Kingdom

Do you have a pet? It does not need be a bull mastiff or a huge cat; a fish tank with some beautiful neons and other exotic fish can be a great source of peace and interest. I love animals, but not everyone lives in a place that is suitable for dogs and cats but having another living thing in your life can be a source of great happiness, an anchor for single people or families.

Lonely or unhappy? Then choose the right pet for your environment, animals of all kinds can bring a daily smile to all of us.

"They all have distinct personalities—just like us, like people."

Dr. Jane Goodall

Throw a Progressive Dinner

Have you ever been invited or involved in one of those "progressive dinners?" They can be really fun and help to enlarge your circle of friends. This is how it works: each couple, in a relatively close neighborhood, is responsible for cooking, preparing, and hosting one course of a night-long dinner party. One couple has hors d'oeuvres, another the soup course, the next the main course, and the last the dessert.

This is a great way to meet new neighbors, have fun preparing your offering, and host new and old friends at your house.

"Our lives are not in the lap of the gods, but in the lap of our cooks."

Charles Dudley Warner

Be an Armchair Traveler

Make a wish list of places that you would love to visit—Los Angeles, Las Vegas, Rome, the French Riviera, or perhaps Africa or the Brazilian rain forest. Then start planning your dream.

Buy some good travel guides that tell you about the main attractions as well as those little-known off-the-beaten path places. Plan to stay in your dream vacation town or city for at least a week—I know too many people who have crammed "most of Italy" into a week. To my mind, that is no way to really get to know the place of your dreams. If you don't have the funds for an actual trip then try the Travel Channel or the Discovery Channel, it is cheaper than a ticket.

"Get a subscription to a good travel magazine. It is the next best thing to being there."

Shhh . . .

I believe that true clarity of thought can come from being alone and not distracted. A quiet house at midnight can be an oasis of rejuvenation. Everyone needs solitude sometimes. Being with people, whether it is co-workers, family, or friends, all of the time does not give us time to be alone and to contemplate our lives, our choices, to take inventory of where we are, and to assess our priorities.

We should not feel bad about wanting to be alone. Sometimes a quiet house or apartment lends itself to some much-needed, deep introspection. You owe it to yourself so try to arrange it.

"The ticking of the clock became my only distraction. It was a bloody good quiet."

Dr. Margaret Whaley

Get Down on Their Level

Build an "indoor fort" with your kids, I remember doing this with my two boys and we had so much fun. All we needed was dining-room chairs, sheets, and a couple of blankets. Then we got into it, played cards, and pretended we were escaping thunder-storms—cozy, fun, and inventive.

We only did this on days when it was better to be inside than out. Once we kept the "fort" up for a whole weekend and my kids actually sent "mail" and gave our fort an address!

"It's fun being a kid."

Bradford Arthur Angier

102

Come On, Get Happy

Create Your Own "Greatest Hits"

If you have a collection of old LP records why not convert them to audiotapes or burn your favorite selections onto CDs, do it for yourself or even a friend. So much of what we listened to in our college dorms is not available on commercial CDs so make your own with the CD burner on your computer.

What a great rainy-day activity, re-recording favorite tunes for yourself and for a special friend.

"Bring over some of your old Motown Records . . ."

Rod Stewart and The Temptations

Let the Wind Give You Direction

Learn to windsurf. If you live or vacation anywhere near a lake or the sea there are almost always windsurfing boards and sales for rent. Many places also have people to teach you how to do it.

Try something new, have an adventure—windsurfers, they say, "have more fun!"

"I'll try something new . . ."

Smokey Robinson

Love Fresh Juice?

Have you got a blender? Most of us do, so why not rummage through the refrigerator and create your own smoothie? Or plan it, go to the market and buy some bananas, berries, maybe some vanilla yogurt. Use your imagination.

Don't forget to add ice cubes or ice chips to make it instantly cold. Start blending ice, juice, and fruit and get creative, what about a little peanut butter?

"Doubtless God could have made a better berry, but doubtless God never did"

William Butler

Scrap it!

Make your best friend a scrapbook for their birthday. If you have been friends for long, you probably have drawers or shoeboxes full of memorabilia to paste into a "this is your life" memory book.

If you need photos, or other materials to make it really complete, ask other mutual friends what they have. Make something for your friend to treasure forever.

"Memory is the diary we all carry about with us."

Oscar Wilde

Come On, Get Happy

Let the Sunshine in

If you don't already have one, rent a convertible, put the top down, pack a lunch, and fill the car with the family and a full tank of gas. Make it a windy, warm, family day or take friends who like to feel the wind in their hair.

Take the back roads, stop in an antique shop, and don't forget the sunscreen.

"So free we seem, so fettered fast we are!"

Robert Browning

When in Rome . . .

If you live in a fairly large town or city, or you are visiting one, pick out a museum from a magazine or visitor's guide. Do something you ordinarily wouldn't do. Go to a natural history museum, a science museum, or art gallery.

Surprise is a wonderful thing, perhaps you and your family will find new interests, or ask new questions, talk about your new experiences.

"She came out of the theater chattering like a magpie. I couldn't remember what the play was about, but I did appreciate the enthusiasm."

Della Cortez

Write Some Fan Mail

Did you particularly enjoy the performance of a singer, dancer, or actor recently? If you really admired their talent and ambition, tell them how you feel. So what if you never get a response or just get an autographed photograph as a "thank you." The fact that you took the time to write with praise and enthusiasm for their work is reward enough.

"Compliment is something like a kiss through a veil."

Victor Hugo

Don't Forget the Bug Repellent

My idea of camping was an upgrade to a suite at a Ritz Carlton while visiting another city. We have camped out a few times and come home with great stories (such city-slickers, we), and some of the best photographs we have ever taken.

How to Enjoy an Outdoor Shower—that is going to be the title of my next book. Not because it is strange or sinful to get naked with a bar of soap underneath a hose but oh, it was the coldest water ever, one degree less and it would have been ice.

**"Happiness depends, as Nature shows,
Less on exterior things than most suppose."**

William Cowper

Funny Time for a Picnic

Most people have had a cookout for dinner (or lunch), maybe at the beach or park. My parents loved to have a cookout early on Sunday mornings in a beautiful nature reserve and park not far from our house. They would pack the eggs, bacon, coffee, and frying pan, and off they went. It seemed oddly exotic, eating breakfast out, in a park, deserted except for us "odd balls."

Now here is the really strange thing about our cookouts. Although we were teenagers when my parents got the idea, and you know how teenagers easily sleep until noon on most Sundays, we really loved these early mornings. My favorite family photos were taken at that park during those early morning breakfasts.

"I did it my way."

Frank Sinatra

Don't Let Your Favorite Things Go up in Thin Air

Sometimes I just can't help myself, when I read or hear something so compelling, so special, I must share it. Such has been the case with many things, but two stand out in my mind because these experiences come up in conversation often.

The first is my recording of Maya Angelou, the great poet and novelist, when she addressed thousands of people on Dr. Martin Luther King Jr.'s birthday, some years back in Minneapolis. It was aired on the radio and a great friend recorded it for me.

The other is a verbatim audiotape of Bailey White's *Mama Makes up her Mind*, a collection of extraordinary short pieces that have been loved my many millions.

"Make happy those who are near, and those who are far will come."

Chinese proverb

Try it You Will Like it

When you are in a new restaurant, especially one that serves ethnic food that you are unfamiliar with, take some chances and choose something that you have never tasted before. It could be a great culinary adventure.

Our kids love to try new things and are mostly pleasantly surprised by their adventure—except once, when Mike ordered a large platter of smelt (tiny oily fish). He braved it out, though, and ate quite a lot of them.

"There is no such thing as a little garlic."

Arthur Baer

Rent a Classic

Rent the classic movie *To Kill a Mockingbird* and show it to your kids. It is not a cheerful or "fun" movie, but it is life-changing and a true experience.

"Fun" is not always "fun" just as "happy" is not always "happy," not in the conventional way. But *To Kill a Mockingbird* is a movie that will enrich you and your family. It is a film of total "humanity."

"Great moments that change your world are so varied, so prize them all."

Rabbi Ezra Shottenstein

Come and Get these Memories

At the turn of the next year, take your new calendar and do something you may have never done before; if you have, hooray for you. Record all the birthdays, celebrations, graduations, and anniversaries of all of your good friends and family members. My aunt was great about this and she never missed my birthday. Even one of my best friends, Ed, remembers my kids' birthdays this way.

How happy can you get? Well, if you remember someone's "special day" you will guarantee mutual happiness.

"Forget-me-nots—the flower, the memories, the way you say I love you."

Anonymous from a greeting card

Just a Touch Goes so Far

"Lip service," perhaps a phrase with bad connotations, but kissing a friend's cheek is a kind, uplifting, and welcoming way to "break the ice."

Watch how world leaders greet each other. Many of them kiss one another on both cheeks, it is a show of trust and kindness. Should we adopt this? I think so.

"Respect may be shown by adopting other people's customs. It is also a sign of solidarity."

Emily Post

Open up and Say . . .

Have you ever had to speak at school, church, a business seminar, or other such gathering? When you are facing a group of stuffy, seemingly intractable people in an audience, start by loosening up the crowd with some humor—self- or audience-deprecating one-liners can have them in the palm of your hand almost instantly—they will be grateful for the humor.

Humor can be a tool that opens up a world of possibilities, don't let a room full of grumpy people dissuade you from being the clown. It will turn the audience around for the better, and what is more fun than making people laugh?

"Humor is the great equalizer."

Anonymous

A Garden Of Any Kind Says "Yes" to Life

Grow your own kitchen herb garden. You can do it in the middle of a city or deep in the countryside. It is simple, either buy your favorite seeds or some stores sell them already growing in their own pots.

Clipping fresh chives into your home-made soup is a treat, so is adding fresh basil to tomatoes and mozzarella. Serving fish? Reach for the dill. Fresh is always better.

"It's a good thing."

Martha Stewart

May I Call You Back?

One of my favorite lines from *Seinfeld* is when Jerry is interrupted by a phone solicitation. Instead of getting angry with the caller, he simply says, "I'm busy now, but could I get your number and call you back later?"

We all get a little edgy about being interrupted at mealtimes or on the weekend, but perhaps we should take a hint from Jerry, and meet those irritations with some humor rather than anger?

"Well, if I called the wrong number, why did you pick up the phone?"

James Thurber

Treat Them with Respect

Splurge on a pair of slippers; get the ones with real lamb's wool interior, and suede uppers. Treat your feet to a little luxury; if you have a job that has you standing most of the day then you know you owe it to them.

Going barefoot is OK in the summer or in warm climates but in the north, where it gets cold, your feet need comfort and protection from the wind, snow, and cold kitchen floors.

"Feet are considered a delicacy among certain animals, you know . . . In fact, there are certain man-eating animals who will eat only the feet, leave everything else, will not touch one other thing."

Blake Edwards

Try a Pint or a Bushel

Go berry picking. There are many farms that allow you, for a fee, to pick your own favorites—blueberries, strawberries, raspberries. You will get the feeling of the "harvest," and that will make the eating of your bounty all the sweeter.

When you get home with your bounty, try this: wash the berries, let them dry, and refrigerate them. After an hour or two, take them out and mix in half a cup of cranberry juice and half a cup of orange juice, let the berries soak for about an hour before eating. If you are a purest, however, eat them on the way home.

"The pie doesn't lie. If the fruit is fresh, you know."

Betsy Robbins

Come on, Get Happy

Seek and Ye Shall Find

My kids loved scavenger hunts. My wife and I would hide crazy hints all over the house and they would just giggle with glee. The "prize" was really no prize at all, just a common household item, but it was sleuthing for them that was fun.

We made some of the clues in rhyme, with a word missing, and sometimes we drew pictures. Almost twenty years later, I have kept some of these clues and they still hold warm memories for me.

"The richness of life lies in memories we have forgotten."

Cesare Pavese

122

D.I.Y. Cereal

Make your own granola, breakfast bars, or morning cereal. It is not hard and can be a lot of fun. Go to your favorite health food store or any market that has fresh, organic whole food such as nuts, spices, oat, and wheat germ. Buy a scoop of all your favorites.

Dried fruit and raisins are plentiful, and can be found at most stores. Raw oats may be a little more difficult to find, but if you are determined, you will find all of the ingredients you want. Surprise a friend at breakfast one morning with your own "home recipe" cereal.

"Home-made. Always better."

What Is Your "Top Ten?"

Get a group of friends together. Give each of them a piece of paper and pencil, then, ask them to list the top ten songs that are the most important to them, and why.

This may sound silly, but I guarantee this little experience will lead to great long conversations and probably a bit of "disharmony," which won't hurt as long as it is not a diatribe.

"Getting to know someone—is not a task—it's an art."

Pierce LeBlanc

Unwrap a Smile

Put a chocolate on your loved one's pillow, just like they do at "turn-down time" in the best hotels. Why not start the night with a sweet for your sweetie; you can even pretend you are away in a grand hotel.

It is just a sign of caring and love to put a tiny gift on his or her pillow. You will enjoy the unexpected smile that a little piece of chocolate brings to their faces.

"A kiss is just a kiss, unless it's chocolate."

From the *Chocoholics Diet*

Try Cooperation, not Competition...

I have a good friend who, with her husband, teaches their two boys the art of cooperation.

By that, I mean their first inclination is not to "win" but to be "team players." Their kids are taught to see the advantages of being part of the group and of improving the group by doing the best that they can without compromising themselves or other members of the team. These two boys will grow up with strength of character, and we all can be happy to know young men like that.

"We don't care if we don't come home from a long weekend of showing or riding in a challenging horse show—no blue ribbons? Who cares? We had fun."

Christi Cardenas Roen

Get up and Get to Work!

Do you enjoy your job? Is your career giving you satisfaction? Are you happy at work? We spend at least a third of our days on earth "at work." If you are not happy, change it; you can. Don't feel trapped, get out and start your own business, find a place that makes you happy.

Even in tight job markets, you can find something that gives you positive self-esteem; a job you are happy to wake up to. So don't settle, make yourself happy from 9–5.

"Dig your well before you're thirsty."

Harvey B. Mackay

Mirror, Mirror

Don't compare yourself to people who are rich, beautiful, and well connected, what is the point? So what if you feel you are not up to their status. Take stock of your own strengths and list them. You are sure to have a range of strengths and talents that the guy next to you only wishes he had.

When we get into judging ourselves harshly, we come up short. I am never going to be in the top fifty most beautiful people but so what? I have got talents that interest me far more, and give me more satisfaction that I can count. So count yours.

"It's the little things that keep me going. I've lost a lot with the 'big things.'"

Norman Bergman

I Can Only Give You . . .

Do what you say you are going to do. Never over-promise, but live up to what you say you are going to do. Don't let unrealistic promises weigh you down and make it impossible to live up to your goal.

If your promises involve others—you will be happy when you come through for them. Your self-esteem gets stronger and your self-stature will keep you buoyant.

"She offered me safety . . . I gave her home . . . she promised forever . . . and I forgot."

Nathaniel Brent

Come On, Get Happy

I Hear a Symphony

There is a reason why you hear music piped into department stores, elevators, restaurants, and many work places. Music, depending on your taste, almost always improves mood. It has been proved that the audio backdrop of your house, as well as your workplace, has a positive effect on your mood.

I keep music on (my preference is mostly classical) at home, in my car, and at work. It has a calming influence on my general sense of wellbeing and it makes me happy.

"I can't hear you . . . the water's running."

Tom Stoppard

Experiment

Get your hands really dirty; all the way up to your elbows. With what? Clay, I say.

Using your hands to create something in clay—a pot, a vase, candle holders, or just something decorative—is enormous fun, not to mention therapeutic and very physical so you will get a good workout too.

"Fine art is that in which the hand, the head, and the heart of man go together."

John Ruskin

Come On, Get Happy

Try Reveling in Someone Else's Happiness

A good, strong role model for happiness may be just what you need. If you are feeling lost or aimless, look to others to prop you up, it is something that too few of us do and it can certainly lead to happiness.

In Dr. Jane Goodall's remarkable book, Reason for *Hope: A Spiritual Autobiography*, she gave the reader a range of beliefs, things that all of us can do to make the world a better place. This book gives us hope in a world that has changed remarkably.

Reading a book that is so inspirational and intelligent is enormously positive. It is the kind of book that does, indeed, give us hope.

"I was just Oprah's biggest book club member. Wow, what good books she chose. I'm really a new, but devoted reader."

132

Come on, Get Happy

I Did it, I Really Did it!

Take a chance. Dare yourself. Get on the roller coaster. Try one of those crazy rides at the fair or the theme park. You may never laugh as hard as when you are hanging upside down with a couple of hundred other people. Half scared, half exhilarated, these crazy things can bring the kid in you right back.

Don't, however, have the hot dog with "everything on it" or the spicy meatball sandwich just before you buy your ticket as it could make the whole experience unforgettable for other reasons.

"I hated those rides at the fair, but my son, Scott, demanded that I go on the BIG roller coaster. I agreed. What could I do? I loved it, we never laughed so hard together, but I hope we do sometime again."

Gloria Friedberg

Never, "For Granted"

Write a note to a friend or loved one; take five minutes to tell them that you care. Let the surprise make both of you happy. Every time I speak to my sons I finish the phone conversation with "I love you" and I always hear them say the same to me, "Love you too, Dad."

"All the miles between us. Oh, it's good to take, to write, to stay in touch."

Valerie White

My Music May Not Be Your Music

You know how everyone seems to love a "sunny day?" There is nothing wrong with it, but have you ever enjoyed walking in the rain, without an umbrella?

Walking in the rain makes me happy, not during an electrical storm but during a gentle rain. Look up into the clouds. Get soaked. Get happy. Rain gives life. Life is good.

"Try listening to Manuel de Falla's 'Nights in the Gardens of Spain,' to help you love a sunless day or night. Extraordinary, to say the least."

135

Come On, Get Happy

Work it!

Take it to the next level. Unless you have a chronic health problem, you should push yourself just a little harder. Do twenty push-ups every morning. Inch up to thirty, then forty, and so on.

This is not about trying to look totally buff, or about vanity, it is just about getting healthier—feeling better, fighting fatigue, building responsive muscle mass. Just do it, but do it little by little.

"You probably have some financial retirement plan. You should also get your body in shape for the same kind of investment."

Fred Barrows

Get Yourself Some Endorphins

Take a friend to a strange place. If you have a good friend who does not go to the local orchestra, the local theater, or out to any unusual or culturally different restaurants then treat them to a new experience. Maybe they will love it and maybe they won't.

Surprising a friend with a new experience is a gift that makes the friend happy, and also as the giver. Try to make it really unusual.

"Life should not put you in a rut. Skip out at least once in a while."

Sam Levinson

Crazy You Say?

Cut the legs off of your porch furniture. Yes, you read this correctly.

Then suspend each piece (not the tables) from the ceiling with decorative chains and turn them into sofas and chairs that swing!

This may sound crazy, but swinging is a lot more fun than sitting still.

"It's just simply different."

Teri Bennett

As Good as it Gets

While out on country roads in the summer you are likely to come across roadside stands selling fruit and vegetables. Stop and buy some of the freshest most delicious home-grown treats you can imagine.

Cucumber, lettuce, various kinds of tomatoes, green beans, watermelon, cantaloupe, strawberries, corn-on-the-cob; you could fill up your back seat with this great road food and enjoy it for weeks.

"The urge to eat a tomato, just picked, while still standing in the garden, is nearly hypnotic."

Beth Ann Starek

I Can Do It

Break a bad habit. It may not be easy, especially if it is something like smoking, but there may be easier ones you can take a look at and feel good about bringing to a halt—nail biting, knuckle cracking, foot tapping.

If you know you do it, you can concentrate on it, and you can make the behavior disappear. All it takes is self-awareness, determination, and the good feeling of self-worth—you can do it!

"The will of man is his happiness."

Friedrich von Schiller

Give, Until it Helps You Too

Pick out your favorite non-profit business or community charity. Offer to bring your expertise to the board of directors—you may have great knowledge and experience that they can use. Don't sell yourself short, give your experiences away for the better good of your special interest.

Happiness sometimes can be just plain giving. Non-profit organizations always need a hand, if not a head, so offer yours and make a few like-minded friends in the process.

"The smile on that beautiful hungry face was so bright and red as it gets."

Cindy Birdsong

Get out There on Some Blades

Go skating. You don't have to have the most expensive and fastest in-line skates, use your old ones. Oil them up and get out on the sidewalk (don't forget your helmet). It is fantastic exercise and a way to capture just a bit of your childhood. Get your partner out there too; what a way to spend a Saturday afternoon.

If it is wintertime, and you live where there are "natural ice rinks" then ice skate instead. Take your time if you are rusty, getting up on those blades can be a lot of fun.

"I've got a brand new pair of roller skates, you've got a brand new key."

Melanie

It's Just the Way I Remember it...

See that playground over there? Yes, the one that is nearly empty? Now it is your turn, no matter what your age, to get on the swing, climb the jungle gym, and to get a partner for the see-saw.

We sometimes forget the simple joys we had as kids on those schoolyard amusements so why not knock off a few years and take a run at the slide?

"No more brilliant than sunlight is a child's delight on a day at the park."

Marion Rose Tofte

You Have Made Me so Very Happy

Tip a really good waiter or waitress way too much. I have had wonderful experiences in restaurants: impeccable service, perfect food, and unforgettable experiences.

It is not about over-spending. It is about showing those who have served you how much you enjoyed their caring, smart, inventive way of showing you a good time. You can then leave the restaurant with a smile on your face, not just because the food was great but so were the people.

"If you care, prove it."

Anonymous

Email-Free, and Happy About it

Send postcards, not necessarily just while you are away. Send cards with just a few lines on them telling a good friend what you are up to. There are beautiful cards available—museum shops carry great cards.

In an age where email rules, I look more and more forward to old-fashioned mail—the kind you get from your mailbox. The kind you read and re-read, and probably keep in a shoebox after you are done reading.

"What a warm, nice gesture—the handwritten note or post-card. The human touch lives on!"

Carolyn Ross

Worth the Price of the Ticket

My sister-in-law, Nina, just loves theater, and wants to see as much of it as she can. She is not big on expensive seats, just great theater—home-grown high-school productions, original writers showcased in various venues—she enjoys all types of theater, and it is infectious.

People she knows, friends and family members, always get the "low down" on what is good, what is worth the price of a ticket, and frankly, what is not worth your time. She is a "thumbs up" theater aficionado.

"Lifelong interests are life-saving habits."

Dr. Ken Flemming

Keep the World Alive

Instead of buying a pre-cut Christmas tree, buy a small live tree for the holiday. After the festivities and when you have removed the decorations, keep it alive in the pot.

In the spring, find a great place to plant it and you will always have a Christmas tree in your yard. Try this once—or just do it for a number of years. They will be living testaments to happy Christmas' past. I recently saw one of my family's trees, some thirty years after planting it and it is at least thirty feet tall.

"Let Christmas live on, and save trees at the same time."

"Laugh, I Thought I Would Die"

Go to the library or bookstore and pick out some audiotapes of your favorite comedians. Eddie Murphy, Al Franken, Jerry Seinfeld, and Louie Anderson, to name just a few, can make a routine trip to work or a road trip all the much more enjoyable.

Laugh your way to work—a great way to start the day, and end it too.

"Water cooler humor, be the most admired guy at the office, retell what you just listened to."

Don't Overanalyze

Sometimes we start trying to find layer upon layer of reasons for things that happen to us, or things we instigate. I say, if you are happy leave it alone. Don't question the source, just go with it!

It is not always important to know "why." If we ask too many questions, sometimes we get too many answers.

"Happiness is a mystery like religion, and it should never be rationalized."

G.K. Chesterton

149

Come on, Get Happy

Stick up for Free Speech

Do you know what "Magnetic Poetry" is? They are kits containing numerous, small, magnetic strips with a single word printed on each one. Using these you can compose your own poetry on your refrigerator. Invite the family to add, subtract, and create a "giving poem."

This can not only be a hilarious pastime but, even better, possibly create an interest within a family member to really get interested in poetry—a wonderful path to the world of words.

"Every man has the heart of a poet."

Alfred Steinmetz

Don't Catch the Cell Phone Bug

Turn off your cell phone. Use it for emergencies only. I am in a business that demands that I use the phone, almost without pause, for eight to ten hours a day. But I refuse to use the cell phone in the car, at anyone's home, or in business meetings.

My cell phone is for outgoing calls, only four people have my number and that is for emergencies, not just idle talk. Free yourself up, turn it off!

"After about two weeks go by, and the obituaries are published, the phone calls and faxes slow down—just a little bit."

Johnny Carson

Don't Let Yourself Forget

A few years back, I quietly took my parents' old 8mm home movies and had them put onto videotape. I gave them the tape for Christmas and it certainly brought back a lot of great old memories from film that was close to becoming dust.

Those camping trips in the 1960s, Christmas, Easter, and Thanksgiving; film fragments contain long-forgotten moments in the life of a family—a real treasure.

"Gone, but not forgotten . . ."

Anonymous

Sleep with the Window Wide Open

Do you sit in a stuffy, fresh-air starved workplace all day as so many of us do? The glass office-towers in big cities can almost make you feel refrigerated in the summer and much in need of real, fresh air.

So, at night I take delight in sleeping with the window open. Fresh air pours in even in the winter and I believe it promises a deeper, more restful sleep. I know that the air is cleaning, especially after eight hours of "manufactured" oxygen.

"Real rest, deep sleep, comes only with real night air."

Wally Sullivan

153

Come On, Get Happy

Mow a Lawn or Plant a Tree

Do it for a friend, yourself, or your family. Do it for free. Do it because you love life of any kind, and you can give this as a gift of life to anyone with a little plot of land.

Getting your hands dirty with earth creates a special kind of kinship with life. Planting a tree is life affirming and a physical evidence of hope; it is freeing and loving and it makes us feel better for having done it.

"The miracle is this—the more we share, the more we have."

Leonard Nimoy

Give in, Once in a While

Once in a while have a large cheeseburger with lettuce, tomato, mayonnaise, onions, mustard, and ketchup. Don't forget the fries and the milk shake and don't feel guilty, enjoy it.

This is a real happy meal, if ever there was one. But remember, too many of the "happy specials" can cause unhappiness so you have got to know where to stop, easy now.

"Have it your way!"

Burger King tag line

Get Your Handwriting Analyzed!

I once went to a party where the host had invited a handwriting analyst for some very interesting fun. This woman worked for the local police department, and really knew her stuff. With a little trepidation, I wrote the words she dictated, and signed my name.

I was astonished at her ability to "read me" through my not-terribly-elegant penmanship. She had me dead-on and spoke to me mostly about my strengths—I am sure she saw more than that but it was, after all, a party.

"First, know thyself."

Diogenes Laërtius

Forget-Me-Not

If you pack a lunch for a loved one—kids, husband, wife, whoever—don't just put a peanut butter and jelly sandwich and cookies in the bag. Add the most important part of the lunch, a note, just say "have a great day," or "good luck on the math test," or even just "go get 'em."

My mother, many years ago, put little notes in my lunch box when I was in grade school. They were thoughts from all over the map. Some were funny, some just said "I love you, see you at 3 pm." I never shared those notes with any of my lunch mates, they were mine and they made me unashamedly happy.

"A smile is a lunchbox. Pretty clever, I think."

Come On, Get Happy

Watch Out for Drips!

I just bought my third box of Popsicles—I don't care if I am middle aged, I love them. They are sugar-free and delicious, and I don't know why I'm defending buying or enjoying them.

Cherry is my favorite. What is yours? You cannot dislike a Popsicle—unless it is banana-flavored, that I understand. Don't be afraid to pretend you're chasing the "good humor" man, we are never too old for that pleasure.

"It's like ice cream that's gone to heaven . . ."

Pepperidge Farms

Wave Your Freedom, and Your Happiness

Fly your national flag, it is a testament to the good feelings you have for your country—and it is also decorative, festive, and beautiful. There is nothing wrong with showing "your colors," there are many positive things about the country you come from so celebrate them.

"Patriotism is not so much protecting the land of our fathers as preserving the land of our children."

Jose Ortega y Gasset

If You Are Aware, Peace Is Everywhere

Do you know what a prayer plant is? It is a beautiful flowering plant that opens, or blooms, in the morning and closes at night. It is a beautiful, simple plant and there is a sense of peacefulness about it.

Simple things, like a prayer plant, can give us so much "quick joy." In the end, it really is the simple things that make us happy.

"It is nature's beauty that both mystifies me, and speaks volumes of unalterable truth, and peace."

Helen Victor Ryan

Be a Mentor

Whether it is within your church or school, kids who come from broken homes or who are orphaned need positive role models to show them the way. To give someone a character to look up to, to emulate, is a gift, a two-way gift.

A busy friend of mine; newly married with a full-time job and lots of interests, recently surprised me by mentioning that he had a young boy he was mentoring. He takes him to baseball games, helps him with his homework, takes him out for a hamburger, in short he is an adult friend. How my admiration for my friend grew at that point.

"I thought you cared. Now I know it . . ."

Jared Dimondstein

161

Come On, Get Happy

Celebrate Rites of Passage

Have you ever been to a bar mitzvah, or a bat mitzvah (the Jewish rites of passage for boys into manhood and girls into womanhood)? They are beautiful ceremonies where the honored child reads from the Torah and learns special prayers that speak of lifelong tenets and morals.

Attending either ceremony is enriching, fascinating, moving, and healing. Whatever your faith, these are extraordinary moments where families come together to celebrate life's progressions.

"The dance of age, the upholding of passages, is a gift from God."

From a speech by Rabbi Harold Bloomfield

Teach Your Children Well

Teaching your children to be financially independent and responsible is invaluable—it ought to be taught in schools. Nathan Dungan writes about this in his best-selling book: *Prodigal Sons and Material Girls: How Not to be Your Child's ATM*. It has at it's core a three-word guide, "share, save, spend." This is a great reminder about how to consider money, share being key.

Sound, sensible advice about the value of money and the value connected to the spending of money is fundamental and something that kids everywhere need to know about.

"Share, Save, Spend—in that order."

Nathan Dungan

Change Will Do You Good

Knowing when to leave a relationship, a job, a friendship is good. Sometimes problems are irreparable, things fall apart and our center, as it is said, "cannot heal." Don't be careless or thoughtless about making this decision but there is sometimes a time when you must say "goodbye."

It is important to be aware of how your relationships, of all kinds, are affecting your life. Some are toxic and you cannot "fix them." Knowing this is freeing, empowering, and ultimately a choice that leads to happiness and freedom.

"T'was better we parted . . . the light had died . . . and we would have too."

Oliver Taylor Jackson

Made Too Much Popcorn Last Night?

Then make popcorn balls with the leftovers and turn watching a movie into a sweet treat.

Use just enough white Cairo syrup, and heat it. Mix the syrup with the popcorn, and form into balls. Wrap each one individually and chill.

"This is one time when it's okay to lick your fingers."

Stop the World . . .

For some of us, being "alone" is very difficult. I am not talking about being a hermit, I am just talking about a quiet evening without company, no place to go but your sofa, no TV or radio, maybe just some soothing music and a great book. Nothing feeds one's mind as heartily as a good book.

"Listen to your heart. Your mind will follow."

Jeremy Dykstra

Put up a Butterfly Feeder

Buy a butterfly feeder, those little boxes that you often find in garden centers. They are great for attracting beautiful, winged beings that brighten your garden and your attitude.

We live in a world of beautiful, amazing beings. I am a nature lover and you can be too, this is a great way to incorporate a little more nature in your own backyard.

"We must remain as close to the flowers, the grass, and the butterflies as the child is who is not yet so much taller than they are."

Friedrich Nietzsche

Take the Weight off

Have you harbored the weight of having done something you knew was wrong, or that caused pain to someone or their reputation? All of us have, because all of us are human.

As humans we are fallible, but the emotional weight can be lifted if we go to that person, and simply own up to what we have done, make amends, and ask for forgiveness. What a way to get very happy.

"From listening comes wisdom and from speaking comes repentance."

Italian proverb

Tighten up

This is going to sound weird, but it does really work. If you get out of bed with puffy eyes and drooping lids get a large bowl, fill it with cold water, and add several ice cubes. Let it stand for five minutes while you make your morning coffee or tea. Now, lean over the bowl and submerge your face in the ice-cold water. Hold it in there as long as you can, towel dry, and repeat if necessary.

Many people do this religiously and it really works. Under-eye bags recede, frown lines tighten, and you also wake-up very quickly.

"God, it's cold, but it sure works."

Barbara Anderson

Happiness is Recycling

Once a month, take all the magazines you have managed to accumulate and drop them off at your local retirement home, you will be cleaning up your place, and giving other people lots of good reading.

Looking about daily lives we can see lots of excess. Hoarding magazines after I have read them used to be one of mine, but not anymore!

"A new kind of recycling—one that makes other people happy."

You Are Never Too Old to Take Piano Lessons

I have, like millions of people, lamented not sticking with a musical instrument. I copped out of piano, and have long regretted it. The journalist and writer, Noah Adams, wrote a splendid book, titled, appropriately enough, *Piano Lessons*. It chronicles a year in his life while he learnt to play the piano—from the Steinway Showroom where he purchased it, a great story in itself, to the day he . . . well, I'm not going to ruin it for you, go and buy it, you'll love it.

Why not take up the instrument that you would love to learn to play. As they say, it is never too late—just ask Noah Adams!

"What is vibrato anyway?"

171

Come on, Get Happy

. . . til You Drop

Throw an "oldies" party. If you are like me, you have held onto the old 45s that were, in my day, the equivalent to CDs. Invite your friends and serve up the food from that era—Lipton Onion Soup Dip, corn chips, Coke, 7-Up, and pigs-in-a-blanket. Put the singles on the turntable, and dance, dance, dance.

My collection is largely Motown, great songs that influenced a generation and bring back some wonderful memories.

"There's always room for JELLO."

Old ad for JELLO

Wiggle Those Toes

A true sign of summer are "flip-flops," "thongs," "stringers"—the rubber sandals that we take to the beach, the pool, the gym, and anywhere where it is warm.

When your toes can get all-day air and you cash-in your socks, that signals, to me, the relaxed summer months to come and that's happy!

"I've still got sand in my shoes . . ."

The Drifters, *Under the Boardwalk*

173

Come on, Get Happy

Light Your Fire

Laying the first fire of the autumn is a welcome kind of ritual. When it is crisp and windy outside, building a fire is such a great feeling. Use seasoned dry wood, good kindling, and some newspapers to get the first flame then savor that great smell that permeates the outdoors while you sit, transfixed by the dancing flames.

Birch is beautiful, but burns quickly; oak is a great hardwood and lasts a long time. Pick your own favorites, they all have their own, great aromas.

"Fierce fire reveals true gold."

Chinese proverb

Ten Things You Should Not Ignore

Do you know what a reflexologist is? It is a person who specializes in massage of the foot—one of the most sensitive parts of your body, and also one of the most stressed and commonly ignored. Spending a little money on your metatarsals can change your life, not to mention your attitude.

Our feet take a daily battering so treat them right and get a foot massage, it will be an unforgettable experience, perhaps even habit forming.

"I live for foot massages. I actually save up, so I can get one every month. I'm not kidding."

Bea Smith

Celebrate with the Past

Find a wedding picture of your parents—try to find one that reveals them in a more natural, less posed way. Then, for their next wedding anniversary, have the photo framed—sterling silver for their twenty-fifth or gold plated for their fiftieth and in between use your imagination and some good taste.

There are so many gifts you can commemorate an anniversary with, be imaginative. This is just one idea but is guaranteed to be one that is treasured.

"We did this for my parent's fortieth anniversary. I never saw both of them cry at the same time—with joy."

Peggy Anderson

Crush Some Ice

OK, we are going to make snow cones.

Take out the ice, rev up the blender, the food processor, electric ice crusher, or just grab a hammer. Crush the ice and pour your favorite flavors liberally on top—cherry soda, lemonade, cola, vanilla cream soda, limeade, all of the above.

"Any season is a good season for an old-fashioned snow cone."

Television That's Good for You

Have you ever watched the program *NOVA*? It has been on for years in the U.S. and you can't go wrong watching this program. It is fascinating, brilliant, entertaining, and habit forming (a good habit).

You can feel good about watching this reality television. There are no bachelors searching for the most beautiful woman or people eating earthworms, just fascinating television.

"Check your local listings."

TV guide magazine

A Real Happy Meal

It is cold and raining, the wind is whipping up and you are indoors, looking out. So why leave, stay in and make a big pot of the best home-made soup ever.

Bundle up warmly and go out to your favorite market. If you need to follow a recipe, copy it, and take it with you. Alternatively, do what I love to do and make it up as you go through the aisles. Get everything fresh, organic if you can—beets, carrots, celery, fennel seeds, other root vegetables, tomatoes (these can be canned), vegetable stock, beef or chicken, garlic, maybe some white wine or red wine, depending on what your preference is. Have fun with it. The whole house will smell welcoming to all who are expected for dinner, and don't forget the bread!

"Chicken soup for the soul."

Bestselling inspirational book by Jack Canfield and Mark Victor Hansen

I'm up to it and I'll Prove it!

People without clear goals tend to be aimless and at a loose end. This can be frustrating and can also produce anxiety so set some goals for yourself—tone up your body, start a reading club, volunteer, improve your performance at work. Having goals helps to focus you and to create order and harmony in your life.

Make a list of what you would like to accomplish by the end of the year. Maybe you won't hit every goal, few of us do, but you will have some fun trying.

"His eye is on the sparrow, and I know He watches me."

From an old Gospel song

Nine Things to Be Happy About

Here are several summer things to be happy about:

- ☀ Rhubarb and strawberry pie
- ☀ Ice cream on a hot night
- ☀ Ice
- ☀ Iced tea with a sprig of mint and or lemon slices
- ☀ Grilled steaks
- ☀ And/or grilled vegetables marinated in your favorite salad dressing
- ☀ Sand in your shoes
- ☀ Outdoor showers
- ☀ Sun-block

Let's face it, almost anything we do in the summer, short of digging ditches, is something to look forward to.

"We just got here."

From *We Just Got Here* by Carly Simon

181

Come On, Get Happy

"Happy" Is a Live Concert

Live music, wherever you hear it or see it performed, is one of the great joys of life. Whether it is your favorite country and western, a heavy metal band, or your local orchestra, live music is just so rejuvenating and exciting.

The emotional experience of being in the audience and listening to your favorite music is wonderful and you will talk about it the next day, and the next, and the next—who can blame you?

"Ladies and gentlemen, please help me welcome . . ."

Host and Announcers

I Can't Believe it Is You, We Haven't Talked in Two Years!

Keep in touch with relatives. So many of us live in distant towns and cities and staying in touch can be a real problem when you are miles apart, even by air.

My aunt was great at not letting distance come between family members. She did it the old-fashioned way and wrote letters, sent cards, clipped interesting things from her local newspaper and sent small, but meaningful, gifts on birthdays. She was the glue that held all of us together. Why not designate yourself as the hub of the family—it is a gift to give yourself and everyone else.

"I buy stamps in big quantities usually $40 worth, and note cards. I can't pass a stationery store. But I think it's a good habit. Keeps me away from the computer and the phone."

Barbara L. Thompson

Where Do I Sign up?

Did your family ever go for an extended hike and sleep beneath the stars? Camping can be so much fun and many places, all over the world, have wonderful campsites with running water and hot showers. Maybe you caught the camping "bug" when you were a youngster and you went to "sleep-away" camp. It is a great way to meet new kids, learn to swim, play various games, and just take in the outdoors, a wonderful way to bond and make friends for life.

"There is nothing like waking up to a hand-warming roaring fire".

Tom Lechler

Get Your Fingers Working

Okay, everybody, it's time to get your fingers covered with paint—young and old, kids, Dads, Moms, grandparents, you can all get in on the act.

Buy some cheap paper, put it down on a table, open the jars of finger paint, and get your hands dirty! Great works of art are not always created with a pen or a brush.

"New traditions—now that makes me happy."

Make a Batch Of Energy

Take a handful of raisins, a handful of mini pretzels, a handful of dried apricots, a handful of wheat, a handful of dried apples, and a handful of malted milk balls and store in an air-tight container. I love trail mix, especially on a hike with a cold bottle of water. It is a high-energy treat that you can easily make for yourself. If it is stored carefully it can last for months.

Chex mix is good too, a real classic, although a little salty. Try mixing raisins, cashews (unsalted), dates, and dried apricots for a really special "break from the path."

"Crunch your way through a great hike."

Legendary and Unique, a Gift for Yourself

One of my favorite gifts to give, and one that is relatively inexpensive, is a subscription to *The New Yorker*. Before you think it is a snobby gift, take a look at the current issue. Inside, there is something for everyone—fascinating personal profiles of both the famous and not so famous, poetry, great fiction, and wonderful political conversation. It is always a pleasure and always a surprise. Another brilliant and clever magazine is *Punch*, published in the UK. It has been around for many years, and for good reason, and contains great writing, and brilliant wit.

Oh, and of course the cartoons. Once a week you almost always find yourself clipping out a good one and adorning your refrigerator or sending it to a friend who you know will really "get it."

"If I could only read one magazine, this could be it."

Come On, Get Happy

"What Will You Have?"

Open up a soda fountain in your kitchen. Do this on a special occasion or for visiting company.

This is what you need:

- A blender (for milkshakes)
- Several kinds of ice cream
- Club soda (for genuine egg cream)
- Malted powder (for malts, of course)
- Crushed nuts
- Bananas
- Berries of your choice
- Cherries
- Whipped cream
- Straws and long spoons
- Plenty of napkins

Sometimes it is more fun to stay home and get creative than getting into the car and going out for a treat, this way you can experiment too!

"Don't forget the napkins. You'll go through about 2000 of them."

From a Dairy Queen advertisement

Come On, Be Resilient

Do not let minor obstacles get in your way. Most roadblocks are minor and you can usually be clever enough to maneuver around them.

Say to yourself, "Yes I can," and, no doubt, you will. Everything is in your attitude and your willingness to bounce back, maybe even higher than you were before.

"Fall seven times, stand up eight."

A Japanese proverb

189

Come On, Get Happy

Man's (and Woman's) Best Friend

My family loves dogs and we have had a number of them, each with their own distinct personalities. Dogs are extraordinary beings. They are loyal, open, able to learn, and sensitive to the moods of their masters and the family as a whole. They depend on you, and the beauty is, in turn, you know that you can depend on them too.

Treat yourself to a day at a dog show. It is great fun to see all the breeds and to watch them compete. The owners are also worth watching, a kind of "side show," if you will.

"Dogs never lie about love."

Jeffrey Moussaieff Masson

Live Your Dream

We have a good friend who, after one faded marriage and with four grown children, decided to move to France. Certainly not a woman of great wealth but nevertheless a registered Francophile, she had the audacity to leave her comfortable home and take a chance—what an adventure it was.

She ended up staying for a year and came home with a lifetime of memories, stories, and fantastic photos. She treated herself to a fantasy year away so why not give this one some thought yourself? Passport up-to-date?

"Risk has its rewards."

Evil Knieval

Any Reason to Celebrate

Have you ever heard of "half birthdays?" These dates are demarcations of six months prior to your next birthday. Not surprisingly, our kids always wanted us to celebrate their "half birthdays" so we would go out for dinner or for ice cream on these dates and they loved it. It was not their real birthdays, but I think if you can find any reason to celebrate, do it.

Only the other day I reminded my twenty-three-year-old son of his half birthday and he said, "oh yeah, let's go out to dinner."

"Our birthdays are feathers in the broad wing of time."

Jean Paul Richter

Plan Early for Great Gatherings

If you live alone make sure you have plans for any and all the holidays you observe. Being alone on Christmas Eve or the first night of Passover is not only a prescription for self-pity, but depression as well.

Buy Christmas presents in July, pick up small, amusing, inexpensive birthday gifts throughout the year. If you see something "perfect" for a new friend, don't hesitate, buy it and put it aside for a special surprise. Make sure your friends and family know that you would love to have them over to your place, or to join to them at theirs for the holiday. This does, by the way, include your birthday.

"Celebrate! Celebrate! Dance to the music!"

Song lyrics from *Celebrate*

Read My Lips

Films with subtitles are great for those who love to learn about the world in general and get involved in an engrossing story at the same time. If you don't live in a large urban area that has what are sometimes referred to as "art houses" (theaters where foreign films are featured), you can join an on-line video club and rent some wonderful, life-expanding movies.

"Photography is truth. The cinema is truth 24 times per second."

Jean-Luc Godard

"I Love You, Now Change"

Remember when you first fell in love and why? What did your new love offer to you? Acceptance, some call it "unconditional love," is the key to moving forward in any good relationship. Accepting others for who they are is not always easy. It demands that you look past certain attitudes and behaviors they may have that you do not necessarily approve of or agree with. Trying to change someone's basic behavior is difficult at the best of times, impossible most of the time, and is a great anxiety producer for both you and them.

Learn to let people be who they are. Ultimately, it will free you up to be all the things you want to be. Try changing things in your life, not in others.

"The art of acceptance is the art of making someone who has just done you a small favor wish that he might have done you a greater one."

Russell Lynes

Customize, Customize

Try going to one of those shops that customize T-shirts to your specifications. Imprint a shirt with one of your own, unique observations, perhaps a nickname or a code that only you and your friend or partner know how to crack.

Small, personal gifts that have been planned or made unique for a friend or partner are great, and they make everyone happy.

"Happiness is a choice that requires effort at times."

Anonymous

Once a Year Is Better Than Never

Many people think that Christmas or holiday letters that go out to friends and family are corny, but I don't. I like to keep up to date with what the prior year served up to people I know. Even if you only make the effort to reach out and tell your loved ones what has been going on once a year, it is a sign of an ongoing bond and one that I look forward to.

Every time one of these missives arrives, I am taken by how little I know about what happened to friends just months ago. It does, however, make me feel "caught up" and that is a happy thing.

"The grand essentials of happiness are something to do, something to love, and something to hope for."

Allan K. Chalmers

197

Come On, Get Happy

Up All Night

After a busy day and a harried week, it is sometimes a private joy to stay up until the small hours. While the house is quiet and everyone is asleep, you can grab some peace for yourself, maybe read a bit, thumb through a magazine, or just ruminate on the day's pleasantries.

We all need solitude, at least occasionally. While I love my family, it is necessary to be alone sometimes; it helps us to focus, and to be at peace with ourselves.

"And the night shall be filled with music, And the cares that infest the day, Shall fold their tents, Like the Arabs, And as silently steal away.

The Day Is Done, Henry Wadsworth Longfellow

Look in Unlikely Places for New Interests

A friend of mine was aimlessly looking for something new to do when he came across a bread-making class and signed up. He loved it and learnt how to make a long list of breads. He even finds a bit of therapy in at least the "kneading process."

Something else he found out is how many new friends he has, not just from the class but also some pretty hungry old friends who are home-made bread fanatics.

"Action may not always bring happiness; but there is no happiness without action."

Benjamin Disraeli

Find Six Perfect Leaves

One of our kids is keenly aware of his surroundings, loves nature, and manages to spot things that the rest of us miss. Every fall, while taking a walk, he will find the first leaf that has changed color. He always finds beauty in simple nature. Not long ago, I visited him at his apartment on his college campus. On his bulletin board he had pinned the first red leaf of last year. It made me feel so good about him, about us, and about life.

Try finding six perfect autumn leaves, press them between heavy books to flatten them, and then frame each one. This way you will have a beautiful reminder of the change of seasons, and one you can hang on the wall.

"It is the marriage of the soul with Nature that makes the intellect fruitful and gives birth to imagination."

Henry David Thoreau

Celebrate New Traditions

Break with tradition or start your own. I have a blended marriage—Jewish (my wife) and Protestant (me). While we are not particularly religious, we have always shared tradition, which, if you think about it, creates a new tradition in itself.

Who says you can't have eight nights of Hanukkah candles and a Christmas tree at the same time? Sharing traditions is a real gift.

"He is happiest, be he king or peasant, who finds peace in his home."

Johann von Goethe

With Pen in Hand

Email is a dangerous, hindering, and paradoxically time-consuming invention. I remember writing real letters, a couple of pages of my news and daily thoughts; I put it in a real envelope with a real stamp and mailed it. It probably took two or three days to reach it's recipient, but that was the reality not so long ago.

I've started writing letters again, not email, to a couple of friends. No "instant messaging." It gives me a chance to think about what I want to say and the way I want to say it. Writing an old-fashioned letter lets you ruminate about your life and what is at hand in the life of the person to whom you have written. It is a much more satisfying act and a kind of gift to the writer and the addressee.

"I've kept all of my father's letters. I cannot part with them."

It Takes a Village

A family is a community, of sorts, which is why it is so important to teach our children what community means at home and as early in their lives as possible. Little tasks that contribute to the family community can be seen as real contributions. Setting the table, taking out the trash, clearing the table, doing the dishes. It is not about "work," it is about creating a healthy, happy family.

If parents choose to ask their kids to contribute to the daily chores, they will make them feel like important components of a community. And this will give them a sense of wellbeing.

"Happiness is not a destination. It's a method of life."

Burton Hillis

I Don't Know What it Is, But I Want the Recipe

One thing that can be really fun is to call some of your friends one afternoon, or on a weekend, and have an impromptu potluck dinner. Each guest brings something they can throw together—remember this is about fun not work—and a reason to get together. Sometimes not planning ahead makes for a more memorable time with good friends and good food.

Bring the kids along, or houseguests if they happen to be visiting, a couple of videos, a volleyball, and home-cooked food; nothing could be better.

"The best way to cheer yourself up is to cheer somebody else up."

Mark Twain

Surprise a Fellow Worker

Stop a co-worker, not necessarily someone senior to you, and compliment them on their work—"you really brought a lot of creativity to the Smith program" or "wow, what a great meeting, you really did your homework." What a difference a humane workplace makes in one's life.

It is so easy to find something positive about something someone has done in the workplace. Let them know, make them proud and happy.

"Good humor is one of the best articles of dress one can wear in society."

William Makepeace Thackeray

205

Come On, Get Happy

Invent Something!

All of us at some time have said: "I wish I'd thought of that," but maybe we can invent something ourselves? Think of the things that you use everyday and say to yourself: "There has got to be a better way."

Read the "New Patents" column for inspiration, there are inventors all over the place so put on your thinking cap and use your creative juices to invent! What a great way to get happy.

"What one man can invent, another can discover."

Sir Arthur Conan Doyle

Try Walking Away

Take a real break from work; have a cup of tea and maybe a scone or small sandwich with it. Relax, take the heat off for twenty minutes, lean back and enjoy your cup of relaxation. Interruptions at work are so healthy for us and they make us more productive and happier people.

Try a different tea every once in a while. There are some excellent herbal teas that really are magically mood altering. Although coffee has its place, it tends to speed you up so try tea and learn to treasure those few minutes with it.

"Maybe it's not so terrible that there's a Starbucks on every corner in America."

Make a Wish

Give what you can, even just a few dollars, to the Make a Wish Foundation, an organization that grants "last wishes" to children with terminal diseases. Or perhaps the Ronald McDonald House homes for the parents and other family members of children who are being treated in hospitals far away from their own homes.

I have a real problem seeing children in bad situations, partially because I'm an over-protective father but also because I just hate seeing kids in pain—who doesn't? Giving to either of those organizations is a real win-win.

"Most of the important things in the world have been accomplished by people who have kept on trying when there seemed to be no hope at all."

Dale Carnegie

Make Some Home-Made Happiness

Make your own lemonade, don't buy it frozen or bottled from the market.

Here is how you do it—if you have kids or grandkids, or somebody else's kids, it is even more fun:

- ☀ One quart container
- ☀ The juice of nine lemons without the seeds
- ☀ ½ cup of sugar
- ☀ About ¼ of a quart container (250 ml) of ice
- ☀ Enough water to bring it to the brim

You could even make some money by setting up a lemonade stand in your neighborhood. Alternatively just sit back, sip, and enjoy.

"A smiling face is half the meal."

Latvian proverb

Go for a Sleigh Ride

Whether you live in a town or in the country, weather permitting, rent a sleigh, driver, and horse and have a wonderful ride through new-fallen snow.

Don't forget to pack the lap blankets and the hot cocoa, it makes the trip that much more enjoyable, then snuggle up to the guy or gal next to you.

"Sleigh bells ring, are you listenin' . . ."

Walking in a Winter's Wonderland by Dick Smith and Felix Bernard

You Can Never Have Too Many Friends

Each year try to make one new friend. If your house phone is silent, perhaps you ought to think about why that is. Have you failed to cultivate friendships and make new ones or are you letting grudges get in the way of old friendships? Try reaching out to new people through work, your health club, church, synagogue, or wherever you find people who share interests with you.

We all have times in our lives when we tend to pull back and isolate ourselves. There are many reasons for this—grief, loss of a spouse, clinical depression—but people can help, and many will be eager to if they can. Making new friends or reinvigorating old ones can renew you and your life in amazing ways.

"When you make the finding yourself—even if you're the last person on earth to see the light—you'll never forget it."

Carl Sagan

Wash Out Your Mouth with Soap

We live in a world where every third phrase has a four-letter word for emphasis. All this profanity has become so common that it has become accepted, what used to shock now merely bores. So why not go against the grain and rid your vocabulary of vulgarity? It is not that difficult and it will renew your world-views and de-sour your outlook on life.

Break the mold of the usual street language that permeates our lives. Get past the need to be demeaning to everyone else, and ultimately to yourself!

"Bad habits are like a comfortable bed, easy to get into, but hard to get out of."

Anonymous

Keep Your Ears Open

Learn to listen. People often say interesting and thought-provoking things and they reveal themselves through great conversation, even jokes and the recounting of their own family history. One of the most wonderful evenings I can imagine is one where I just sit back and listen to friends.

Of course, conversation is about give and take. Don't act like the sphinx, join in, ask leading questions, get personal. A great joy in my life is really getting to know someone and drawing them out.

"Listen or thy tongue will keep thee deaf."

American Indian proverb

Visit a Petting Zoo or a Working Farm

Talk about happy, I love both of these activities. Taking the children, yours or a niece and nephew, to a petting zoo is great fun. The children become wide-eyed at petting a calf, goat, or lamb. Sometimes there are pony rides, too.

When visiting some working farms as a guest, you are often expected to join in—collect new-laid eggs, fork out some hay, or help milk the cows. It is a hands-on pleasure to experience what the farmer does daily to put food on our tables.

"But I freely admit that the best of my fun I owe to horse and hound."

George John Whyte-Melville

Ever Said: "I Haven't a Clue?"

Must we have an opinion about everything? How about just sticking to opinions on things that we actually know something about? These days, in the age of "super information," we seem to be expected to know something about everything. Whether it is popular culture, global warming, N.A.S.A., you name it, we are supposed to know it all.

The fact is we are too over-committed to know so much. Let go of the notion that we need to be so impossibly "plugged in." A simple "I don't know much about Russian impressionist painting," might just free you up to have a real conversation.

"It is salutary to train oneself to be more affected by closure than by praise."

W. Somerset Maugham

Do You Know When it's Time to Go?

Sometimes you know, in your heart, that it is time to say "good-bye." Whether it is a friend, a pet, or partner, sometimes the best thing to do is just say "goodbye." Often it is hard to know when the time has come but, if you go deep within and ask the hard questions, often goodbye is the best thing to do.

Saying "so long" is hard and you have to work out if it is right for you so think about this one for a while before you act.

"Knowledge of the self is the mother of all knowledge. So it is encumbered on me to know myself, to know it completely, to know its minutiae, its characteristics, its subtleties and its very atoms."

Kahlil Gibran

Don't Pass the Fruit Stand!

Ah, the first, sweet, delicious peach of summer. Part of the joy of the whole summer experience is biting into it and letting the juice drip down your chin and your arm. There are many varieties of this fabulous fruit but why not just pick the most ripe and ready peach you can find and enjoy.

Summer offers so many great things to be happy about, this is just one but it is one of my favorites.

"Talk of joy: there may be things better than beef stew and bake potatoes and home-made bread—there maybe."

David Grayson

Make a List

Sometimes it pays to take what some people call a "personal inventory," especially if you feel down or depressed. Take a sheet of paper, or your journal, and record all the positive things in your life. Name those who love you, great times you have had, special gifts you have been given, times you've nearly died of laughing, your faith and what it means to you—you will find the list is almost endless.

There are millions of people on this earth far less fortunate than ourselves. By taking stock of what we have, not just the tangible things, it helps to put our lives and our moods in a good perspective.

"The unexamined life is not worth living."

Socrates

Get Ready!

Start collecting your winter firewood early this year. Whether you use a chain saw or a regular handsaw, get started during the summer. Cut down bush for kindling and split your own logs. If you don't have trees that need trimming, then drive out into a rural area and find a farmer or landowner who would like some of his land cleared.

It is hard but basic work, no-nonsense exercise that you will get at least two benefits from.

"Progress lies not in enhancing what is, but advancing toward what will be."

Kahlil Gibran

Pick up the Pieces

Do you want to create something truly unique? Go to a quarry where there are odd-shaped or broken pieces of granite lying around and pick up one that really appeals to you. Buy a raw pedestal or metal frame and voila—a one-of-a-kind coffee table.

Use marble polish and file away any sharp edges. It is easy to put together and a real conversation piece.

"Remember how in that communion only, beholding beauty with the eye of the mind, he will, be enabled to bring it forth, not images of beauty, but realties."

Plato

Make Way for the New

Do a thorough inventory of your old CDs and LPs. Box up the ones you just don't listen to anymore and take them to a store that buys and sells used records. By cashing in on the old ones you can buy some new ones or perhaps that boxed set that you have been wanting—a great way to recycle old, tired music for new.

"Maybe one day it will be cheering to remember over these things."

Virgil

221

Come On, Get Happy

If it's the Last Thing You Do . . .

Try this alone or with a friend. Write down as many as fifty things that you want to do before you die. Skydiving? Enter a swimming contest? Eat a whole pie? Go to your place of worship each weekend for a year? Take all the neighborhood kids for ice cream? Spend a month in Paris? Ask yourself "why not?" Not just "how would I ever."

"Happiness is possibility."

Anonymous

Keep 'em Laughing

Make people laugh and release some happy-making endorphins for you and others. Making people laugh is good for you, good for them, and just plain good. Not everybody is a clown or verbal acrobat, but repeating great jokes, or remembering a great Seinfeld or I Love Lucy episode is fun, and fun is good.

Lighten up and tell a joke or two. I have a small repertoire of favorites, so cultivate one of your own, and keep 'em laughing.

"Laughter is the shortest distance between two people."

Victor Borge

Ever Hear Of Unconditional Happiness?

We have all heard the term "unconditional love." It is a wonderful concept, but what about those of us who fear showing happiness or taking delight in thoughts of flight or "unconditional freedom of thought?"

Don't censor your happiness, bring it out in the open, share it, it is infectious.

"Most people ask for happiness on condition. Happiness can be felt only if you don't set any conditions."

Arthur Rubinstein

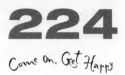

Regress!

Introduce shadow puppets to your kids—that is where you cast a light against a wall, make the rest of the room dark, and create the look of all sorts of creatures with your hands.

Don't just do the wolf or dog, get inventive. Your children will love this little bit of magic in the dark.

"There are so many ways to show how much you love them . . ."

Jack Stack

Give Your Time

Surprise a friend or a loved one with the gift of time. Ask them out for coffee and sit with them for however long they have time to talk. Listen to them, talk about their life, their family, whatever they want to talk about. Give your time as a gift. Keep yourself out of the conversation—it is their time, be there especially for them.

We are all way too busy. "Email me," "fax me," "hope to see you soon," "it would be great to meet, but I'm just too busy right now." Our time, what we can give of it, can be of great value to a friend, family member, or anyone who just needs an "ear." Time, it has been said, "is the greatest kind of any wealth." Give it as a gift to someone you care about—it will be a happy investment for both of you.

"Words (and time) can sometimes, in moments of grace, attain the quality of clouds."

Elie Wiesel

Sing it, Baby!

Take voice lessons. Maybe you have been complimented on your singing, or maybe not. Learning the correct way to hit all the right notes could be a lot of fun, or even a way to a talent scout. Even if you have no plans to sing professionally, just do it for fun.

"Singing in the shower is the high point of my day."

Lester Macmillan

Touch That Dial!

Try a new radio station in your car or home. You might be surprised and find a new favorite, it could be a country and western station or an oldies station. Variety broadens our lives and makes us more interesting so that should make us all happy.

"Change is good," as the saying goes. Maybe not always, but often it is, so at least it is worth your time trying.

"I've got a list of varied favorites as long as my arm. I love to check out all kinds of music."

Harold Lincoln

I Think I Can, I Think I Can, I Think I Can . . . and By Gosh, I Can!

You will never know unless you try, and trying is what life is all about. You may sometimes have to stick your neck on the block to find out but the exhilaration of risk-taking can, in a way, be its own reward. If you have got an idea, and you think it is a good one, putting it to action will only make you happier.

Start something, don't be meek about it, get out there on the field.

"The difference between the impossible and the possible lies in a person's determination."

Tommy Lasorda

Walk Your Talk

Sometimes the best way to make someone happy is to be honest with them. You don't have to be brutal or demeaning but telling someone your honest opinion, even though it may waver from theirs, is a kind of gift.

I believe, that by doing this, you show a greater respect for the other person. It also shows that you care about your relationship with them.

"T'was her thinking of others that made you think of her."

Elizabeth Browning

Practice Random Acts Of Kindness

I don't like it when people say: "Have a good day," it is mindless, although good-intentioned. However, I do believe that starting the day with the best possible attitude does give us all a "personal best boost." If you get out of bed with a negative attitude, the day will eventually prove you right. So, instead of just saying "Have a nice day," somehow, someway, make sure that person does.

"When I give, I give of myself."

Walt Whitman

Soak it up

Hot enough for you? If you are not lucky enough to have a back-yard pool or a community swim club, hook up your hose to a sprinkler, put a lawn chair right on top of it, sit down, and cool off. Invite a friend and sit there together, soaking up the sunshine and the water—cooling and simple.

Who cares what the neighbors think, maybe they will follow suit and join you in a backyard soak-a-thon.

"If I could stay wet, and a little bit wild all the time, life would be sweeter."

Michael Reid

The Backyard as a Beach

Create your own backyard seafood treat. You don't have to be on Martha's Vineyard or Cape Cod to have a great time and create fantastic food. Call your favorite seafood shop or supermarket and ask what is in season—clams, oysters, lobster? Don't forget the corn-on-the-cob and the coleslaw.

If you have never steamed a lobster or roasted clams, don't worry it is easy. Try going online to *The Food Network* or buy one of Bobby Flays' cookbooks; *Book Meets Grill* is a good one for learning the secrets of the Yankee beach cook.

"Tell me what you eat and I will tell you what you are."

Anthelme Brillat-Savarin

Be Ready for Some Happy Surprises

Sometimes, when we try too hard, we miss the little things that can make us happy. Some consider surprises to be unwelcome but I don't think they are. Most surprises are good ones and can make us very happy, if we let them.

☀ Surprise—an old friend dropped by.
☀ Surprise—I found my favorite T-shirt that had gone AWOL.
☀ Surprise—I got two free movie passes.
☀ Surprise—my favorite pasta is the special tonight.

"Happiness often sneaks in through a door you didn't know you left open."

John Barrymore

A Perfect Way to Start the Day

Get up extra early on Sunday morning and don't wake your partner. Go to the kitchen and, quietly, create a special breakfast for two. Bring the trays to the bedroom with the Sunday paper and gently wake him or her with a real surprise.

Who wouldn't want to greet Sunday morning with a bowl of fresh berries, toast with special jam, *The Book Review*, and, your favorite guy or gal next to you.

"It's really, when you come down to it, the simplest acts of love—the touch, the look, the mere hand-in-hand that are the most rewarding things about love."

Alice McCombs Ulster

Go to a County Fair

Have you ever been to a real county fair? Not the huge fairs, the small ones in rural areas. They feature home-made goodies—pies, cakes, corn-on-the-cob, a petting zoo for the kids, agricultural exhibits, and even a few fairground rides.

You may not see a superstar singing at the grandstand but you will come away with a wonderful sense of small-town pride.

"We don't remember days, we remember moments."

Cesare Pavese

Stare into Thin Air

Daydream; take some time out of a busy afternoon at work, go to a quiet place, and think about where you might rather be—the beach, your living room, or your garden. Let your mind take you on a quick and refreshing vacation.

We all need a "breather" sometimes. For some peace of mind, take a deep breath, close your eyes, and go wherever you need to in your mind.

"I was a free man in Paris, I felt unfettered and alive. There was nobody calling me for favors and no one's future to decide . . ."

From *Free Man in Paris*, by Joni Mitchell

Put on a Show

Are your kids bored? You too? Are you getting stressed from all the boredom?

Well, as they say in some 1940s movies, "Let's put on a show!" Why not write your own play and give the kids the leading parts. Write some original music and make some costumes.

An original neighborhood theatrical experience can be a great way to get rid of boredom and to have a fun and creative time.

"Hey, let's put on a play!"

Mickey Rooney to Judy Garland in *Girl Crazy*, 1943

It Is Always the Little Things

On Father's Day this year, my younger son, Ross, emailed me a wonderful message. The highlight of the email was a beautiful photograph that he had taken the previous night of a sunset over Lake Mendota in Madison, Wisconsin, where he goes to school.

Getting this, even online, was like sharing the sunset with him. It is a beautiful photograph that I will use as my screen saver and savor each time I see it.

"It's the simple things. I tell you."

Anonymous

Open up and Smile

Ever had flan, a caramel baked-apple, or what about a hot caramel pecan roll? All of these things are made to create smiles. It is fattening and should only be practiced very rarely, but it is fun so try it.

Get everyone in the car and go out for a donut—a fresh, warm, comfort-inducing, sticky, gooey favorite. Go ahead and enjoy!

"I'll have what she's having . . ."

From *When Harry Met Sally*

Live in the Moment

Just this past weekend I visited one of my sons at his apartment in Madison and we spent a wonderful two days together. I vowed, during the four-hour drive there, that I would not get that dreaded goodbye feeling until the moment I had to. This way I allowed myself to enjoy every moment with him—meals, walks, our swim in the lake, and most of all our talks.

"Every minute is precious when you're with someone you love."

Anonymous

Come On, Get Happy

Let a Song be Your Map

Turn off the radio, and sing to yourself in the car. Why sit through ten songs you don't like, when you can sing all your favorites by yourself? Who cares if your pitch isn't perfect or you don't have great stage performance, it's just between you and the steering wheel.

"Belting one out" can be a great way to release tension so tune up your pipes, and just let it go! Singing in the car is almost as good as singing in the shower, but the acoustics are better in the bathroom.

"The song is a tonic for the lost."

Anonymous

The Intimacy of Candlelight is All Yours

Some people think candles are only good for two things: to top a birthday cake or to use during a power outage. This is so wrong, candles can create a wonderful ambience. You can make any room in your house a beautiful, peaceful sanctuary; a place that becomes your own "quiet place."

Tell people who give gifts that you love candles—of all size, colors, and scents—and you will soon have enough candles to read by. What could be more peaceful than that?

"Trust the light cast by the candle."

Anonymous

Throw a Neighborhood Pool Party

Not everyone is lucky enough to have a backyard pool so, if you do have a pool, invite the whole gang over for some splashing-good fun, and a hot dog from the grill.

Extend the invitation once or twice a year. If you designate a specific day then it will be understood by everyone that it is a special occasion.

"Jumped, or pushed?"

Anonymous

A Little Rain Won't Kill You

In fact, it might just light up a smile. Run out in a rain shower, with your clothes on, and dance around in the puddles until you get good and soaked. On a warm summer's day, why not cool off by dancing in the streets? Just keep a few dry towels by the door and some hot chocolate or tea on the stove for "re-entry."

"Raindrops keep falling on my head."

Song title from *Butch Cassidy and the Sundance Kid*

Be Spontaneous

Why not invite the neighbors over for dinner at the last minute and just throw together whatever you have. Make it a casual, last minute affair, or invite the new neighbors to an unrehearsed meal, get to know them with no pretence, just friendship and good wishes. Use whatever is in the fridge and the pantry, don't go all out, it's about being a good host and a welcome smile at the front door.

"Home-made dishes that drive one from home."

Thomas Hood

Take a Class

Have you ever heard the term "lifelong learner?" Certainly all of us, no matter what age, are lifelong learners, but I am talking about expanding your personal universe by taking a course at a traditional school or a community trade school. It will offer you a way to learn something that you have always wanted to know about.

I have a friend, a woman of "a certain age," who wanted to learn how to take care of her own car—changing the oil, spark plugs, learn how to jump-start the battery, fix a broken belt. She had a great time doing this and is now installing a lube rack in her garage.

"Fill her up."

Sign promoting a local trade school, Globe College, showing a gas nozzle filling a brain

Come as You Are

I was once invited, at about 10 pm, to what is called a "Come-As-You-Are" party. This means that even if you are sitting on your favorite chair in your bathrobe, if you accept the invitation you show up in the bathrobe.

It is all in good fun and it can be interesting to see what people are wearing at that hour. Try it, you will have a ball.

"My closet looks like a convention of multiple personality cases."

Anna Quindlen

Throw an Adult Toga Party!

Remember the movie *Animal House*? It was a fraternity on the wrong side of the tracks, and the law, on occasion. But what fun the toga party scene is.

I am not suggesting that you throw such a wild toga party, just have a Greek-themed party with a toga dress code. Create a groaning board of great classic Greek and dance the night away.

"Too much of a good thing can be wonderful."

Mae West

Turn on a Light and Look Towards Morning

Night can either be peaceful or a dark dream that visits us and makes us concentrate on things that are negative or sad. When you have a night like this, you need to remind yourself that the sun will come up in the morning.

In the morning, for whatever reason, our problems and "imagined" stressors seem to come into focus. Keep your eye on the morning, your sadness and anxiety will lessen as soon as the rooster crows.

"A loyal friend laughs at your jokes when they're not so good, and sympathizes with your problems when they're not so bad."

Arnold H. Glasgow

Notice the Full Prism of Life's Colors

Be happy, there is an extraordinary variety that people, situations, and life in general has to offer. Life is meant to be lived in color; the whole palette and every hue brings us a new aspect of opportunity and learning. Be an artist in your perceptions.

Shades of gray are the true colors of life. When you think only in black and white, you miss so much, and judge too harshly. Life is about nuance, not exactitude. People are fallible so don't judge everything with a razor-edged eye because what you see will not be accurate.

Life is about "somewhere in the middle." Nothing is as clean as we sometimes want to see it, so don't look at yourself and use two paintbrushes, one black and one white, look for the grays in you and in others.

"I've looked at life from both sides now."

From *Both Sides Now* by Joni Mitchell

If You Have it Don't Flaunt it

Life is an equal opportunity experience, we are all in the same leaking boat and we need to be aware that ultimately the same things that make the less fortunate happy are the same things that make those with more means happy too.

Sometimes I am amazed at how people openly flaunt their wealth and their social status. Then I remember that I have also been boisterous and a braggart myself. And then I rethink the whole equation. I think back to when I have behaved like that— diminished another by self-aggrandizing something I have done, said, or acquired. I remember again how embarrassed I felt at how I had behaved. What really makes me happy now is hearing about other's fortune and their happiness.

"Retirement, we understand, is great if you are busy, rich, and healthy. But then, under those conditions, work is great, too."

Bill Vaughan

Keep the Kid in Your Heart

Grown-ups sometimes forget to play. I love to play as much as I love to laugh, play means a whole range of things and I am not necessarily talking about bringing out Barbie or Action Man, or maybe I am!

We need to keep our sense of play intact. A buoyant spirit is the key and also the daring to go back and remember the joy of play and imagination.

"When I grow up, I want to be a little boy."

Joseph Heller

253

Come on, Get Happy

The World According to . . .

Treat yourself to the following: a read (via paperback); a listen (via audiotape); to two of the most wonderful, insightful, funny, collections of short stories you'll ever read (*Mama Makes up her Mind* and *Sleeping at the Starlite Motel*, both by radio commentator and novelist Bailey White). What an eye and sensibility this writer has as well as a crazy, offbeat sense of humor, you will be an instant fan.

"A little self-disclosure: she's my friend. I'm her fan."

"Boy, Did I Miss You Today"

Sometimes, we forget our partners are so dear to us. We walk in the door, throw our keys wherever, slip off our shoes, and barely say a word, if anything at all.

If you come home to her or him and you are self-involved and exhausted, remember this: Your partner needs you to "disengage." You don't have to keep working or thinking about work, you are home now, with the one you love.

"Honey! I'm home."

Ward Cleaver

Cogitate

Don't make "snap" decisions. Give yourself time to ruminate and examine—what is positive and what is negative? Are you really ready to make a decision? In our current world, we are asked to do everything instantaneously, even to make important decisions, and this need not be so.

"Must every decision be made at the snap of a finger? Mull things over 'til your decision seems right, and ripe."

Virginia Stanfield Hope

Make New Friends on the Court and the Field

Play some pick-up basketball. "Hoops" with strangers, or let's say, "new-made friends," can be a great release of tension and a great way to sweat your way to health. If you are more inclined to football, then put on your soccer shorts, and get out there on the field. Pick-up football games can lead to good friendships.

This is not something limited to men alone, women can also join in or perhaps start a neighborhood league of their own; the aim is to make new friends.

"I love to see the black kids, the Latinos, and the white kids all playing a game together. The court is a place where race has no place."

257

Do it on a Budget

Are you bored with the way that one of your rooms looks? Do you feel like change but don't have a large budget to make the changes? Try buying just enough paint for one wall, paint it a dramatic color, go overboard, and have some fun with it.

Paint your wall red, orange, olive-green, why not? Make this small change and see how it enlivens the whole house. Another cheap thing you can do is to turn that decanter you have been saving for years into a beautiful small lamp, perfect and not expensive.

**"And all the loveliest things there be
Come simply, so it seems to me."**

Edna St. Vincent Millay

Learn to Juggle

We juggle everything else in our lives so why not have some fun and actually learn how to juggle properly? Start with lemons or limes; don't get too fancy too early on. The main reason to learn this is to let off steam, to learn some new hand-eye coordination, and to laugh. Who knows, maybe you will get so good at it that you will be hired out for children's birthday parties—you might even run off and join the circus!

"Don't start learning by juggling knives. Bad idea."

Anonymous

Join the Local Museum

There is almost always something interesting going on at your local art or history museum, take your pick and join in. You can get discounts at the museum shop, sometimes invitations to opening night parties, and you will also be supporting the "arts."

You never know where this might lead, maybe to new friendships, a new-found love of painting or sculpture—another door to the world opens, and invites you in.

"The artist is not a special kind of man, but every man is a special kind of artist."

Ananda Coomaraswamy

Jump!

One of the most rigorous kinds of exercise, great for the cardio-vascular system, is jumping rope. It engages just about all of your muscle groups, and the funny thing is it is fun!

Hey, if professional boxers jump rope to get in perfect shape then maybe I should be jumping rope too. I see plenty of men and women at my gym jumping rope so get the rhythm.

"Go ahead and Jump."

Jump! by Van Halen

Just Like the Poster

Have you ever stood underneath a natural waterfall on an exotic island? There are many of these natural wonders in the Caribbean and the Hawaiian Islands. It may not be something you can do this afternoon, but you can plan a visit. It is romantic and exciting and, oh yes, well worth planning and waiting for.

"Niagara Falls: the second biggest disappointment to the newly wedded wife."

Andrei Codrescu

Go Hot-Air Ballooning

Have you ever wondered what the world looks like from a hot-air balloon? What a great adventure. There are many places where you can try this out so don't always just wonder what it would be like, gather up your courage, buy a ticket, and drift up and over the countryside.

"Up, up and away in my beautiful, my beautiful balloon."

Up, Up and Away performed by The Fifth Dimension

Sun-Dried

On a warm, windy day, skip putting your newly laundered sheets in the dryer and hang them out on the line to air dry. There is a difference, when you bring them in they will smell totally fresh and free of perfumes or fabric softener.

This is the way to really enjoy a night's sleep, with the residual sunshine from the previous day permeating every thread of your freshly and naturally dried bed sheets.

"Like a sun shower on a hot day. This is one of life's little pleasures."

Go White-Water Rafting

I have a number of friends who say that their biggest thrill, both physically and euphorically, has been white-water rafting. There are a number of places to sign-up, and a number of levels of intensity, pick the level that is suitable for your skills, your ability to swim, and your expectations. The guide at the facility will be very helpful, so have a safe (and wet) trip!

"It was just amazing. I'd do it again, I think we all would."

Belle Newton

265

Beautiful Sanctuaries

Have you ever thought of taking a tour of some of your town's places of worship? There are some beautiful churches, synagogues, and temples where I live and most are welcoming to visitors. Take a day or two, choose the one's you really want to visit, and enjoy their art, architecture, and peace.

Many of us have travelled in Europe, or in other places in the world, and toured the local cathedrals, mosques, and Buddhist temples. Don't forget what is right in our own backyard, it might surprise and delight you.

"The Duomo in Florence: one of the world's greatest architectural wonders."

Rabbi Ronald Fischman

You Can't Always Be a Winner

Give yourself permission to fail. No one likes or invites failure knowingly, and no one likes to admit failure, but it is part of life, like it or not. We don't all make all the right decisions, meet other's expectations, or reach common goals.

It is important not to merge any failure into the fabric of your life. We are no more "our work" than we are our failures. Give yourself a wide berth when it comes to making mistakes—unless they are life threatening, they need to be forgiven.

"Look at it this way—you have nowhere to go but up. There's some pleasure and peace in knowing that."

Ron Simon

Get Happy, Show Kindness

It is so easy to show kindness, especially to strangers. I was ill a few weeks back and had to make a trip to my local pharmacy. The very busy clerk, took the time to walk the aisles with me until we found the medication that my doctor had recommended, it took us ten minutes.

When she walked me back to the counter she said: "Now listen sugar, you go straight home, take two of these tablets, and get yourself into bed. I want to see you back here in our store soon!" I told her that she had made my day, she had.

"What wisdom can you find that is greater than kindness?"

Jean-Jacques Rousseau

Write Your Own Country and Western Song, Base it on Your Lovelife

I'm not a huge fan of country and western music, but I do like some of it. I especially like the song titles lyrics, which are often very funny and clever. So, every once in a while I tune the radio into a country and western station for some good laughs.

Two of my favorite song titles are: *I Walked the Floor Over You* and *Gladly the Cross I'd Bear*.

"Country music is three chords and the truth."

Harlan Howard

Uncork Some Happiness

Open a bottle of champagne and not just on New Year's Eve. Do it to celebrate having a great friendship, marriage, partner, whatever—think of an appropriate, heartfelt toast. Surprise them with this unexpected ace, it will be remembered with a smile forever.

If you don't drink, buy a divine sparkling apple or grape juice. Some of them are every bit as delicious and celebratory as the real thing!

"I have nothing to celebrate . . . but life!"

Edith Piaf

Time for Reinvention

Try a new haircut, why not? You don't have to cut all your long curls short and it doesn't have to be the height of fashion, just sometimes new is good.

You might be delighted with your new look. Listen to your friends' reactions. But remember, most importantly, you have to be happy with it yourself.

"You look maaahvelous . . ."

Billy Crystal, *Saturday Night Live*

Listen to the Past, There is Much to Learn

If your parents are elderly, or if you're lucky to have grandparents, be mindful of their wisdom. Often, they may give it freely as advice but not all parents or grandparents are so open and some keep their histories to themselves. It is important not to let the thread of life get broken between generations, so ask questions.

How I wish and regret not asking enough questions, or their opinions. My grandmother was certainly wise, she had a wonderful sense of humor and could tell great stories. I am grateful for having known her and asking her questions.

"Wisdom is the reward you get for a lifetime of listening when you'd have preferred to talk."

Doug Larson

C'mon Get Happy, Give Me a Big Hug

If you are a warm, giving, caring person, the chances are excellent that you will attract people with the same qualities as yourself. It is so easy to be kind, try it, if you hug someone, they may be startled at first but my guess is that they will hug back. What is wrong with spreading a little warmth?

"Praise is warming and desirable. But it is an earned thing. It has to be deserved, like a hug from a child."

Phyllis McGinley

All Thumbs, But Your Hearts in the Right Place

Pick out a practical project—perhaps building a table or fixing the leg of a chair—and do it with your son or daughter. I wish I had joined my father more often in his "shop" as I don't have many "habitat skills," to say the least. It is fun to complete a project and to learn something practical at the same time.

Practical things do matter. Self-reliance need not be a harsh lesson, show your kids the joy in being self-sufficient, creative, and handy!

"From trash to treasure."

Decorating Cents

Brisk, But Refreshing

On some hot summer days, the temperature can really get to you. Sleeplessness can creep into your bedroom and make for some restless nights. Here is an idea that will not only make you happy but also cool you off. Take a cool (not cold) shower and allow yourself to drip dry, on a towel, on your bed. You will probably drift off to sleep in minutes. If you wake up and can't get back to sleep, rinse and repeat.

"Just do it!"

Nike tag line

Open Your Door and Let Some Love Shine in

Let people in, especially in times of stress or emotional ups and downs. Don't let yourself become a hermit, cogitating on your misfortune, you need to trust someone else and to let their voice lend comfort and direction.

Call an old, trusted friend. Do some reminiscing. Remember the good times and let them bring you back round; let them be your tonic.

"We stayed up most of the night and I don't think I've ever, ever laughed that hard. Oh, the stories we told one another."

Sandy Richardson

Be Open to Letting a Miracle Happen

Don't always look for concrete answers to things that turn out for the better. Science and technology are amazing and they can help us to live longer and have better lives, but what about the things that cannot be explained by logic. You don't have to be a child to believe in miracles. After all, what is a newborn child if not a miracle?

"We couldn't conceive of a miracle if none had ever happened."

Libbie Fudim

Re-awaken Your Tastebuds

Buy or borrow an ethnic cookbook or a cuisine that you are not familiar with. Choose a dish or complimentary collection of recipes, shop for the ingredients, and surprise the family with a culinary adventure.

One of the joys of life is to learn new things and to experiment. Why not experiment in the kitchen and use your family as guinea pigs?

"Eating: one of life's great joys!"

Lynne Rosetto Kaspar, *The Splendid Table*

Run Yourself Ragged

Have you ever run a marathon? It does not have to be a large, famous one, start at your own pace. If you enjoy it, work up to your local marathon. Take it little by little, the point is to enjoy it, get in shape, and not come in first.

There is also the great bonus of meeting new people with common goals and interests.

"Every journey starts with the first footstep."

Kahlil Gibran

Pass on Good News

Pass on good news about a friend or loved one. Be the one who spreads positive gossip. Good attitudes are created by giving people positive words, it goes a long way to make everyone happy.

Talking behind someone's back suddenly takes on new meaning. Good news should travel faster than bad news and you can make it happen. Go ahead, look for the good in spreading the word.

"Ever hear of happy gossip?—Now you have."

May Adams

Thunder and Lightning, and a Great Night's Sleep

Put a tape of something you really love on the stereo. I have a recording of something called "Distant Thunder," an exquisite recording of a hearty thunderstorm. Next, get comfortable, turn down the lights, relax, and let your favorite tape allow you to drift off into a revitalizing nap.

"Yet cease your ire, you angry stars of heaven!
Wind, rain, and thunder, remember earthly man
Is but a substance that must yield to you."

William Shakespeare, Act II, *Pericles*

Give it a Listen

Don't let criticism get you down. If someone is offering it and it is constructive and meant well, try to take it, it will help you. In order to help ourselves grow and make positive changes we sometimes have to listen to someone who genuinely cares for us. Even if they say something negative, in a way it is a compliment for a friend to be honest.

"If it's painful for you to criticize your friends, you're safe in doing it, if you take the slightest pleasure in it, that's the time to hold your tongue."

Alice Duer Miller

Come On, Get Happy

You Are So Beautiful

You know the song lyrics, there are millions of them from virtually every decade since recorded music, and before. But beauty is not about what is on the outside, most of it, if not all of it, comes from within. Beauty comes from wisdom, depth of character, and kindness,

We know a prominent woman who has become more beautiful with every passing year. For dozens of reasons it makes me happy to see her because she's gorgeous in all ways.

"Some people, no matter how old they get, never lose their beauty, it merely moves from their faces to their hearts."

Martin Buxbaum

Twist the Night Away

Have you ever played a game called "Twister?" It really is fun and always results in extreme and exhausting laughter.

A plastic mat with nine circles in three colors is placed on the floor. You spin the wheel and find out what physical appendage must be firmly planted on which colored circle. Eventually you end up looking like a bunch of interlocking pretzels—great exercise for the abs and the laughter muscles.

"We are under-exercised as a nation. We look instead to play."

John F. Kennedy

On Vacation, Take Time to Cool Out

When we used to take family vacations, especially to large cities such as Los Angeles, San Francisco, Chicago, and New York, we would save one night in our hotel for ordering room service—nothing fancy, often just pizza.

We were a close family. The fun of being together, while in our small hotel room with some fun food, always made us happy—it was kind of like camping indoors.

"Go ahead, stay in. Make an adventure of it. A hotel picnic."

Eat Dessert First

Have you ever heard this: "Life is short, eat dessert first?" Maybe you should just try it, and why not—many desserts are more than just empty calories and refined sugar. What about fresh berries over sponge cake? Cantaloupe with lemon and grapes? Home-made biscuits with real maple syrup? Iced milk in a funnel cone? Yogurt and bananas?

Don't let tradition always get in the way of fun. What is the harm in making dessert the first, or only, course.

"Sometime we ate the pudding before the soup, so wicked were we."

Andrew S. Portman

286

Try Opera

Do you hate opera? Are you sure? Have you really exposed yourself to it? As with many other kinds of music, you may not have heard enough opera to really know what you think about it.

Expand your musical tastes. Take some opera CDs out of the library. Try Madam Butterfly or Carmen, hold off on the German operas until you have mastered and enjoyed the lighter, more melodic works. Remember operas are stories, so read the libretto and find out what they are singing so passionately about.

"It ain't over 'til the fat lady sings."

Dan Cook

Bubble Bath!

Surprise her on your anniversary. Before she comes home from work, or her daily errands, put some champagne on ice, draw a bubble bath, light some candles, and . . .

Oh, and one other touch to add a little romance, sprinkle rose petals on your bed—who wouldn't succumb to those "special effects?"

"What's the occasion? You're home."

Barry White

Clean Out That Closet

Pull out all the coats, gloves, scarves, and boots that you no longer want or that no longer fit you. Pack them up, making sure they are clean and not threadbare, and take them to your local charity. Homeless people go cold on the streets every day and night so give them the warmth of those things that once kept you warm and dry in the winter months.

"It ain't a fit night out for man or beast."

W.C. Fields

Come on, Get Happy

Go with Your Gut

Sometimes just guessing can give you the "right answer." Don't feel deficient because you don't know everything, who does? A thoughtful winnowing of what facts you do know may lead you to the answer you are looking for.

Don't be afraid to "ponder." Take time to think things through, to weigh and measure. Snap decisions are not always the best decisions but often you will find your first guess was the right answer. I like to think that we need to think some things through, and others, well, shoot from the hip.

"I shot from the hip, and hit the big time, big time."

Morris Fanyion

Give Yourself Peace

Create a Zen garden, somewhere harmonious and a place to meditate. Get some sand and a rake, find some large and small stones, and make a space in your backyard that reflects the peace and openness of the Zen mind. Arrange the stones and sand in a way that is pleasing to you. It is a creative way to give your home a center, a heart.

"A garden is a lovesome thing, God wot!"

Thomas Edward Brown

Expect the Unexpected

Remember that life is not a series of disasters or major successes. Life is a mix so keep your expectations in check. You will undoubtedly be a happier person once you understand that life is a hybrid of good, bad, and something more from in the middle.

Many of us get frustrated by things that are beyond our control or prediction; if you learn to be resilient and realistic you will be more at peace and ultimately happier.

"Trouble is the common denominator of living. It is the great equalizer."

Ann Landers

C'mon, Get Sloppy

A passion for order can poison the soul. I believe that spontaneity is often the mother of invention and happiness. Keeping everything in its place is a harsh and impossible task. Order from pure chaos is important to attempt to attain, but obsession with order is not something that makes anyone happy.

Loosen up, chill; what if the dishes don't get washed until the morning or the trash sits overnight in the can? Have those two misdemeanors ruined anyone's life? Chances are you were having too much fun to worry about order anyway.

"Perfect order is the forerunner of perfect horror."

Carlos Fuentes

If You Love Someone, Get Yourself Behind the Wheel

Offer to be the designated driver. I am not suggesting that anyone should "over-imbibe," but the reality is that some people do, and in any group of friends that are coming together for a party or a night out, one of you should refrain.

If you can say "club soda with a lime wedge" then you need to be the guy or girl who makes certain everyone gets home safely. Making sure my friends are home, in one piece, makes me really happy.

"You'll be very happy there's a competent person at the wheel, if you're not sober. Everyone should volunteer."

Edna Veronis, M.A.D.D.

What if, What if, What if?

Perhaps this curiosity comes with age or maturity but I have got to the point in life where I ask myself far fewer times: "What if?"

Make yourself happy by realizing that there are far fewer things to fear than we thought there were when we were younger. "What if?" just is not the question that it once was, now I say to myself: "What is . . . is" and that gives me peace of mind.

"Happiness does not like the unknown or the 'what ifs' of life. That is a kind of tyranny."

Rex Harrison

Give Yourself the Gift of Forgiveness

Don't try to just "forget," instead do your best to "forgive." Forgiveness is a gift we give ourselves as well as those who we forgive. The weight lifted from our hearts leaves us free, and unencumbered by the chains of harboring anger.

Forgiveness—certainly a happy and ultimately satisfying act.

"Life is an adventure in forgiveness."

Norman Cousins

296

Come On, Get Happy

The Eyes Have it

Do you get sore, bloodshot, and overworked eyes? Instead of reaching for the eye drops, try this. Go to a quiet place, turn down the lights, put on some soothing music, and place thin slices of cucumber over your eyes. After half an hour you will be surprised how revitalized your eyes feel.

"I can see clearly now."

I Can See Clearly Now by Johnny Nash

Break Some New Ground

One of the greatest gifts you can give yourself is introducing your children to new experiences. Mind expanding, memorable, and rich with surprising reactions, our kids see things that we do not and a first-time experience is a good way to ignite their imaginations.

When my wife introduced baseball to our boys, she started a lifelong wonderful pastime to them, and got me hooked, as well.

"A child is not a vase to be filled, but a fire to be lit."

François Rabelais

Put Your Problems in Perspective, C'mon Get Real

Don't let the small stuff get to you. As Richard Carlson's book says: "Don't sweat the small stuff." And he is right.

If we allow ourselves to let the pettiness that exists in everyday life to get to us, it just gets us down. Don't let a smirk or lack of a "thank you" from a clerk get to you, just smile, and let it go.

"A thick skin is a gift from God."

Konrad Adenhauer

Save a Life, from Afar

"Adopt" a child from a third-world country—there are agencies that can connect you to a child in need. You get letters and photos from your "adopted" child so you know that your money is actually going to that child and not a go-between.

What could make you happier than helping children thousands of miles away and perhaps, literally, saving their lives.

"Children . . . the world's greatest natural resource."

Sam Levenson

Read Yourself Happy

The freedom to read what we want, and then the freedom to then discuss it, argue, or disagree with it is something not only to be happy about, but also to be proud of.

Whoever encouraged you to read, your parents or teachers, there is no doubt that it is one of our greatest pleasures and should be denied to no one.

"God forbid that any book should be banned. The practice is as indefensible as infanticide."

Rebecca West

Jane Goodall Fans Take Notice: Take up Birding

Maybe we should think about not keeping animals that truly need their natural habitat to survive. I'm not talking about dogs and cats, but some animals are not meant to be caged, they need their freedom just as we do.

"Birding" is an extremely popular pastime. It is the sport of bird watching, identifying each type of bird, and enjoying them in their natural habitat and surroundings.

"A robin red breast in a cage puts all Heaven in a rage."

William Blake

Crack Some Walnuts . . .

. . . and some almonds, cashews, brazil nuts, peanuts, and pecans. Now add a dab of butter to a frying pan, melt the butter and toss in the nuts. Stir so they get coated with butter, keep the pan on a low heat and sprinkle in some Cajun seasoning so that all the nuts get a coating.

"Bam."

Emeril La Gasse

Call Your Travel Agent...
Now!

I think almost everyone loves to travel, whether it is to the next town or an exotic location. I am proud to say that my family and I have been to nearly every state in the US.

Sitting in your favorite chair, in your house, you can even do some "armchair traveling" by reading books by writers like Paul Theroux, Frances Mayes, or Bill Bryson. This is no substitute, however, for experiencing, first-hand, the accent, climate, and not to mention the sites.

"I live in New Hampshire so I can get a better view of Vermont."

Maxfield Parrish

We Need to Take Our Hats . . .

. . . off to the teachers around the world who dedicate themselves, often for little pay, to fostering our children into responsible, caring adults, a good teacher is priceless.

I have been lucky enough to have been taught by some very involved and dedicated teachers, as have my children and this makes me very happy.

"A teacher affects eternity; he can never tell where his influence stops."

Henry Brooks Adams

Be a Goodwill Santa

Why not work part-time, as a holiday employee, at the local department store? Sure it is hard work, but if anything will test your boot-camp happiness quotient, this job will.

Shoppers may be harried around Christmas, but they may also be joyful. Buying Hanukkah and Christmas gifts may bring out the best in people so it should be a time of joy and "inventive shopping."

"Hello, may I help you."

Overheard in a department store

306

Come On, Get Happy

Go Backstage

Here is something that is as fun as it is interesting. Ask if you can sit-in on a theatrical run-through at your high-school or college theater—this is a rehearsal with costumes and the set.

You may not see the best performance, and it may be interrupted by the director making changes, but it will take you "backstage" and you will enjoy seeing how it all unfolds.

"George, a camel, stepped on the foot of a Rockette; six sheep came off the elevator as three kings bearing gifts got on; human Christmas trees bumped into eight maids-a-milking at the water cooler and an elf came down with the flu."
On the day "Pandemonium Paid a Visit Backstage" at the opening of Radio City Music Hall's Christmas spectacular, the *New York Times*, 29 November 1986

307

Dare Yourself to Be Happy

Sometimes we find happiness in daring ourselves to learn new things, trying something that we have never done before. Challenging ourselves in this way can be enormously rewarding and lots of fun.

Taking a self-dare is mostly a good thing; why not do something new? Life is about learning, change, and living up to our own expectations. So, what are you going to do to get happy?

"Because it's there."

George Leigh Mallory, when asked why he wanted to climb Mt Everest

Share Some Happiness

One of the sweetest, most important joys in life is friendship. I still have friends today from second grade. They are as close to me now as they were forty years ago. I cannot imagine losing them, they are so dear to me.

A friend is someone you can tell anything, and I do mean anything, to and they will not judge you. The phrase "unconditional love" appeals here, and it should.

**"Q: What is a friend?
A: One soul inhabiting two bodies."**

Aristotle

Dream in Happiness

We live in a time when we judge and berate one another constantly, but take a minute to think of what we are capable of. Dreams we held decades ago have become realities because we believed and we wanted to make things better.

Men and women, all over the world, have enabled our kind by finding cures for disease, sheltering the homeless, and feeding the hungry. We are beings that have astonishing power, so often for the good.

"There are many wonderful things, and nothing is more wonderful than man."

Sophocles

Fall in Love

This is an institution that has many definitions. We can become delirious with love, passion, and new-found attention; but we need to be happy, not just OK with our new relationship.

It is also possible to lose yourself with another. Stay happy being yourself, don't give up on the "you" that made you attractive to them in the first place.

"The ultimate test of a relationship is to disagree but to hold hands."

Alexandra Penney

Happiness Can be Found in a Room of One's Own

You don't have to be in a room full of approving people to be happy, or to define yourself. Be alone; get happy without a crowd. Don't be a prisoner to company or big groups of people, get used to enjoying yourself by yourself.

"What a lovely surprise to finally discover how unlonely being alone can be."

Ellen Burstyn

Go at it at Your Own Pace, and Win

Don't try and measure up to other people's expectations; set your own goals, raise your own bar. Don't push too hard either, that only leads to unwelcome pressure.

If we hit the marks we want to, every day or every week, what do we care what others think? It is only ourselves that we need to be happy.

"We don't know who we are until we see what we can do."

Martha Grimes

Hold Your Head up High, But Not Too High

Have you ever met people who seem so confident that they could never be questioned about anything? We probably all assume that they are the happiest of anyone, after all, confidence builds happiness, or does it?

Nothing is what it seems from the outside—the class clown who is the unhappiest kid in class or the handsome single guy, who goes home alone every night because he can't make a commitment to one woman.

"When we are confident, all we need is a little support."

Andre Laurendeau

314

Lend a Hand

Here is something that seems so elementary, so simple, but at the same time teaches us so much: when you need help, ask for it. Whether it is from one of your children, from a co-worker, or from a friend. Ask your kids, it teaches them that adults need help too. It creates in them the knowledge that "help" isn't something that makes us weak.

Help comes in all forms. I feel really good, whether I've asked for it or offered it. It is a good thing to learn and the earlier the better.

"Help! I need somebody! Help! Not just anybody."

John Lennon and Paul McCartney, *Help!*

Gasoline-Free, Retro-Cut

Use an old fashioned, non-gasoline powered handmower to do your lawn. I am old enough to remember these—no smell of gas, no noise that could wake the dead, just a soft threshing of grass to listen to and the gentle feel of the cut grass hitting my sandaled feet.

These old mowers are scarce, although still available. Unless you mow several acres of perfect grass a week, I suggest you get out there with a relic—grass smells great by the way.

"To me a lush carpet of pine needles or spongy grass is more welcome than the most luxurious Persian rug."

Helen Keller

How About Being Open to Others

Logic is interesting, but is everything exact? I don't think so, I think everything is fluid. We need reason, and sometimes we need things to be as absolute as we can make them, but freedom does not call for absolutes, intractable ideas that can be imprisoning.

I love a good, healthy argument, or more accurately put: "A philosophical discussion." I do think life is more fun when lived without the boundaries that some forms of logic impose on us. So, come on, get more flexible.

"I not only use the brains I have, but all I can borrow."

Woodrow Wilson

Light a Candle

Lights go out? No electricity? Hope it's not for long, but why not make it an adventure. Unless you're under a severe weather warning, and must take shelter, turn this lemon into lemonade, and make it memorable. Always make sure you have a variety of candles—scented ones, candles that are colorful, votives—and make sure you know where they are when the need arises.

"If you can make enough light to see your lover with just one candle and a smile, it is enough."

Sandra Longheart Stevens

Don't Paint Yourself into a Corner

So many of us think long term, what is our "five-year plan?" There is nothing wrong with looking down the pike for life's possibilities, but take into consideration the many unexpected things that may pop up in between "now and then."

Try to be elastic in your view of the future. Don't get too "certain" of what is to come. Planning is good. Certainty is mythical. Have fun and be happy.

"Take short views, hope for the best, and trust in God."

Sydney Smith

319

Come On, Get Happy

Let the Sunshine in

Open all the windows in the car, let the wind come in, and enjoy it. Open the sunroof, if you have one, and get some air. Get your hair messed up. Laugh.

Turn up the radio and throw caution to the wind, not with your driving though! Sometimes you just have to say, "To heck with the way I look, I need some air!"

"I listen to the wind; to the wind of my soul."

The Wind, lyrics by Cat Stevens

320

The Love List

Write down, literally list, the attributes of those you love. Does this sound too calculated, almost cold? Just the opposite, from this you will learn what the strengths of your relationships are or can be.

If we take an account of the qualities of our loved ones it will probably spur us on to try to be better partners or friends. After all, we were attracted to those folks for a reason so have their qualities grown?

"How do I love thee? Let me count the ways."

Elizabeth Barrett Browning

Count Your Blessings

Take stock of all the good that you do and say. Give yourself credit for the positive things you give others, helping them to buoy their days. Make positive self-talk a habit.

Living life with a positive attitude makes a big difference in all we do. Be a "glass-half-full" person and spread it around.

"Every day, in every way, I am getting better and better."

(To be said fifteen to twenty times, morning and evening.)

Émile Coué

The Independent Heart

Not all of us are cut out for marriage or lifelong commitment. That doesn't make us social outcasts or misfits, it simply means, in part, that we do not need "another" to define who we are.

Don't let stuffy, old-world attitudes about the "necessity" of marriage dictate what you do with your life, it is everyone's choice so do what makes you happy.

"A woman without a man is like a fish without a bicycle."

Gloria Steinem

Get Off Your Duff

If you never try you will never fail, but how unhappy that would make us? To be creative in thought and action is what we humans should revel in. Being intellectually inept, for whatever reason, does not make us happy.

Get out there and get something going; build a swing, open a roadside stand, play softball. Create something important at work; so what if you don't do it perfectly, who does? Bounce back from the blunders and get back in the game. That is happiness.

"The man who makes no mistakes does not usually make anything."

Edward John Phelps

Cover the Walls . . .

. . . with old sheet music, magazine covers, wine labels, old labels from canned goods, pages from old phone books, get creative.

If you have a special interest, such as old music or record jackets, why not find a wall in your house and paste them up. Apply a layer of varnish and enjoy your new nostalgia museum.

**"Backward, turn backward o' time in your flight.
Make me a child again, just for tonight."**

Elizabeth Chase Akers

325

Come On, Get Happy

Disco!

Sometimes it is just great to lose ourselves in some good music. It is cleansing, sometimes reassuring, and often invigorating. It keeps us mindful that great art can clear the soul of over-wrought negativity. If you were a child in the late 1960s through to the 1970s, then maybe disco music turns you on . . . right on, right on . . .

Pick out a favorite piece of music, whatever it may be, and decompress with an at-home concert, something that always makes me happy.

"Why waste money on psychotherapy when you can listen to the B Minor Mass."

Michael Torke

Remember Why You Fell in Love

I don't believe in "love the one you're with." I think it is an irresponsible and dishonest attitude. Think, instead, about why and how you fell in love with the one you chose. Take a look at him or her and remember; you probably have a solid, good, maybe long-term, relationship.

Temporary dalliances can be dangerous and hurtful. Take stock of what you have, it is most likely better than anything else you could indulge in and knowing this makes me happy.

"You don't keep running after you catch the bus."

Archie Bunker, from *All in the Family*

Let Nature Take its Course, and Enjoy it!

Too often we want to alter the natural, when instead we should celebrate it and not tamper with it. Mother Nature gave us balance and harmony so let us revel in what we have, even mosquitoes!

We are all a part of life. Nature, in all its forms, makes me happy. It is a never-ending tableau, rich with value.

"In her inventions nothing is lacking, and nothing is superfluous."

Leonardo da Vinci

If They Did it so Can I

Don't let anyone tell you that that you can't do something. Here is the short list of those who haven't let physical infinites stop them from doing extraordinary things:

- ☀ Helen Keller
- ☀ Stephen Hawking
- ☀ Beethoven
- ☀ Michelangelo
- ☀ Stevie Wonder

Care to add? It's all yours . . .

"Monet is only an eye, but what an eye!"

Paul Cézanne

A Shovel Is a Wonderful Thing

When you shovel the snow off your sidewalk, shovel your neighbor's sidewalk too. Here is your pay off: you get the exercise and twice what you would have got if you had only shoveled your half.

I hope you are lucky enough to live in a place that has changing seasons as a natural part of life. Four seasons keep life interesting.

"It takes so little to go the extra mile. I like to think I do go that extra distance for someone, at least once a week."

Shirley North Cottingham

330

Allow Your Parents to Always See You as Their Child

You just have to accept it, no matter how old we get, we are still our parent's children and their role in rearing us never ceases. My eighty-seven-year-old father, after I left his apartment, would call me twenty minutes later to make sure I'd got home OK. It didn't bother me, in fact I took it as a sign of his love and lifelong fathering. Embrace your parents, it is an act of love and who does not find that something to be happy about?

"No matter how old a mother is, she watches her middle-aged children for signs of improvement."

Florida Scott-Maxwell

331

On the Waterfront

Go to a lake with your partner and get out there in a rowboat. It is great exercise, and being out on the open water is always exhilarating. If you are new to canoeing, make sure not to drift too far from shore and don't forget your lifejacket.

Sometimes the simplest things that can make us happy are right in front of us, things that we often take for granted. Spending a day with a good friend in a canoe sounds very good to me.

"Fortune brings in some boats that are not steered."

William Shakespeare

Can You Hear Me Now?

Do you want to be a great conversationalist? Then learn to listen. The best conversationalists are people who speak with both ears, they know their audience, and they are genuinely interested in them.

Express yourself, your opinions, ideas, and sense of humor. Make eye contact, nothing says "I'm listening more clearly" than that, and energize the conversation, make it lively. There is little more fun than a rousing conversation.

"He has occasional flashes of silence, that make his conversation perfectly delightful."

Sydney Smith

Don't Turn a Blind Eye

If you see a need, try and help to correct it—help fill the nation's food shelves, pick up prescriptions for your elderly neighbor, look for a friend's lost dog.

Being anxious about the world's woes does nothing to correct them; action, however, evens things out in little ways. Our involvement in something that has gone awry can get us back on track. Happiness is getting in there with both feet.

"She would rather light a candle than curse the darkness, and her glow has warmed the world."

Adlai E. Stevenson on Eleanor Roosevelt

It Is the Small Things

Housesit for a friend, water their plants, and walk their dog. Feed the fish and leave some lights on at night. Their home is your home and you are entrusted to keep it safe.

Whether it is your hearth or their's, there is something sacred about one's home. Be it a one-room city apartment or a four-bedroom country retreat, we all love the place where we lay our weary hearts.

"Home is where the heart is."

Pliny

Do Something Secret

We have all heard the phrase "random acts of kindness" and I guess that is what makes me happy, that and the afterglow I feel after having done something unexpected for someone.

Call a friend you have not seen for a while and treat them to dinner and a movie—it may rekindle a long-distant relationship. Better yet, arrange, without them knowing, to pay for dinner for them and their partner. What a nice, happy surprise, no need to claim the deed, just do it!

"The greatest pleasure I know, is to do a good action by stealth, and to have it found out by accident."

Charles Lamb

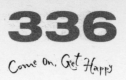

"God, Grant Me the Serenity"

Purity of heart and soul is essentially impossible to achieve but, if you keep certain phrases and words in your daily script, perhaps you will get a little closer to the kind of peace and happiness that we all want so much.

Clear goals, a warm heart, and lifelong guidelines do, without question, make us happier, healthier people. We all need daily mantras to keep us in check, and our hearts and minds open. What could make us happier than words that keep us on a positive road.

"Lord, make me an instrument of your peace! Where there is hatred, let me sow love; where there is injury, pardon."

St. Francis of Assisi (Prayer of St. Francis)

Make the Time, Not the Excuse

We all have interests—hobbies, sports, painting, quilting, cooking—so many different things we enjoy. But too often we don't allow enough time to really indulge ourselves.

Do yourself a big favor, make time daily to do some of the things that you enjoy. It will keep you balanced and happy. Don't let other people's clocks set yours. Set your own goals and stick to them.

"What we love to do, we find time to do."

John Lancaster Spalding

Attract Hummingbirds

My father, many years ago, had two hummingbird feeders (you can often find these at garden supply stores) next to a small fountain, just outside a large window in his family room. When we would go to visit my parents in the summer, it was always fascinating to watch these beautiful birds hover over the feeder and use their needle-thin beaks to feed.

To fill the feeder, just mix sugar and water. Be careful though, these feeders draw bees as well, but so what, equal time right?

"I wish I had the metabolism of a hummingbird, and the appetite of a robin."

Melanie Moore

Curb Your Enthusiasm

Don't push it, go home at 5 pm and miss the rush hour, or at least get a head start on it. Don't set the bar so high that you can't reach it. Don't over-promise, either to yourself or your boss.

Leave some time each day to do your best but not to over-extend yourself, which tends to make you do your worst. Attain balance, know your limits and stick to them.

"Always do one thing less than you think you can do."

Bernard Baruch

Clear Your Mind

Up on the Roof, a rock classic—even in the inner city in the 1960s, The Drifters knew how to "get away from the rat race noise." It is a good lesson. Peace, in this song, was found on the roof of a tenement. Where do you find yours?

I love this song, not just because of nostalgia, but because it speaks of a simple, solution to finding peace in a crazy world, and peace, wherever we can find it, certainly makes us happy.

"When this whole world starts getting me down, I climb the stairs right up to the roof, where all the noise just seems to fade . . ."

Up on the Roof by Gerry Goffin and Carole King

Try Your Personal Best

"Personal best." I like this term because it means that we are aware of others who may run faster, or bowl a strike every time, but we don't have to measure ourselves against other people's "best."

Enjoying a sport, or an activity that calls for "scoring" or "timing," is great, but you won't be happy if you are always competing against other people's "personal best." Be happy with your own.

"I don't care if I didn't finish the marathon. I'm happy that I entered it and ran half of it, anyway."

Porter Brown Jr.

Indulge

Bring home some chocolate to him or to her. What sweet-tooth wouldn't like this surprise? It shows that you have been thinking of them enough to make a "non-event" show of love.

If it is not chocolate then perhaps it is liquorice or four perfect pears. Who cares? This is bliss, this is happiness, and if no one else is at home bring some chocolate home for yourself.

"I felt so down that afternoon, and Bob didn't even know it. In through the door at dinner time he came with flowers in one hand and take-out Chinese food in the other."

A friend

343
Come On, Get Happy

Snowshoe

Snowshoeing—does this sound crazy? Ever done it? It is, in fact, one of the best ways to exercise. If you are lucky enough to live near a place where the snow falls naturally, or even mechanically, it is a strenuous and exhilarating way to get at one with nature.

It can be difficult but you will soon get the hang of it. Try flatlands before hills, it will take practice, it is not just a walk in the park, but wow it feels good.

"Ain't no mountain high enough."

Words and music by Nick Ashford and Valerie Simpson

Stay in Bed

Sometimes you just want to give in to feeling lazy and just hang around in bed. Maybe it is a gloomy rainy day; maybe it is a week-end morning—what is the rush?

I don't think you have to feel bad about not springing out of bed and getting busy. If you have the luxury of staying in bed and covering your head with pillows, go right ahead.

"Lying in bed would be an altogether perfect and supreme experience if only one had a colored pencil big enough to draw on the ceiling."

G.K. Chesterton

345

Clean Your House

Believe it or not, you can have fun cleaning your house and get some exercise at the same time. This is how:

- ☀ Make a pot of coffee.
- ☀ Put on a salsa CD, or turn on a dance music only station.
- ☀ Assemble the cleaning products.
- ☀ Dance while you go from room to room, and make your mop your dancing/cleaning partner.

"Dirt is only matter out of place."

John Chipman Gray

Is this a Snack or Is it Dinner?

You know, good friends and family members don't need you to prepare a fancy six-course meal for them. Unless gourmet cooking is your thing, you may not have to go to great lengths to feed a houseful of guests.

Purchase the following and enjoy:

- ☀ Corn chips
- ☀ Salsa
- ☀ Bean dip
- ☀ Chips
- ☀ Chili
- ☀ Soft drinks
- ☀ Ice cream
- ☀ Paper plates
- ☀ Paper cups
- ☀ Ice

"Life is too short to stuff a mushroom."

Shirley Conran

Looking Good, But Don't Overdo it

Everyone likes to get compliments, whether it is for the way we look or because we are on a new exercise regime. Try to keep a balance and don't get hung up on your looks, remember vanity is a two-edged sword.

"I suppose flattery hurts no one, that is, if he doesn't inhale."

Adlai E. Stevenson

Brew Your Thirst Away

Make tea in the summer, there is nothing so refreshing or natural. Place some tea bags into a large glass container of fresh, cold water. Put it in a sunny place and let it steep most of the day. The sun will gently warm the water and turn it into a mouth-watering drink.

Add sugar if you want to or lemons, limes, whatever you fancy.

"Thank God for tea! What would the world do without tea? How did it exist?"

Sydney Smith

Maintain an Attitude Of Gratitude

Attitude is so important to happiness. It is up to you, in large measure, to keep your spirits up, to keep your eyes on the prize, and to stay as upbeat as you can.

Try setting this daily for yourself: "Don't worry. Be happy."

"No one can make you feel inferior without your consent."

Eleanor Roosevelt

Teach a Parrot to Talk

Think I'm daft do you? Well, I have heard parrots speak with an authority and candor that you wouldn't believe. These magnificent birds are unbelievable mimics and a great deal of fun. They are exotic pets and need special care but if you decide to have one make sure you teach it to talk.

"I'd like to teach the world to sing in perfect harmony . . ."

Old Coca Cola jingle
(by R. Cook, R. Greenway, B. Backer, B. Davis)

351

Come On, Get Happy

Hold the Whole World and Beyond, Right in Your Hands

Where do you want to go today? You can go virtually anywhere when you pick the book that can whisk you away. Travel books, science fiction and fantasy, the classics; get lost in another world, one of your choosing.

"Reading is to the mind what exercise is to the body."

Richard Steda

Act Out

Don't always follow the crowd, think and act for yourself. As Shakespeare said: "To thine own self be true." Do it your way— you don't always have to follow a recipe in, or out of, the kitchen. Don't "color outside the lines" just because you can, listen to your own head and heart and act on your own behalf. After all, you know what happens to lemmings . . .

"A little rebellion now and then is a good thing."

Thomas Jefferson

The Glass Is Half Full

You have to look for a silver lining sometimes, even in the darkest of storms there is usually a bright spot. Be a sleuth and try to figure out what it is.

Most experiences are rarely 100% bad, maybe you can concentrate on the learning experience you will have after it all blows over.

"I'm afraid you've got a bad egg, Mr. Jones. Oh no, my Lord, I assure you! Parts of it are excellent!"

Sir Benjamin Avery

Risk Equals Reward

Taking risks can be enormously rewarding. Try to measure the risk before taking it but, oh, how exhilarating it is once you have taken the plunge.

Make sure that anyone else, who may potentially involved in the risk-taking, knows all about it. Even if you fail it may be a great experience for you, one from which you can learn a great deal.

"I love to sail forbidden seas, and land on barbarous coasts."

Herman Melville

Feel Good in Your Own Skin

How often have we thought the grass was greener on the other side of the fence? That so-and-so has a much better life than we do? From a distance other people's lives can look better but remember, we are all in this boat together and what makes you happy may be very different to what makes your neighbor happy.

"My one regret in life is that I am not someone else."

Woody Allen

Yes You Can!

Take a piece of paper, and write this down: "I am the greatest!" Tape it to your bathroom mirror so that the first thing you see in the morning is a positive "attitude setter."

You have got to believe in yourself and you have got to have the character and the stamina to make it through another day so start off with some positive mental self-help.

"I'm the greatest."

Muhammad Ali

Just Like You Grew it in Your Own Backyard

Have you ever been to a farmer's market? They are pretty extraordinary places, you can get fresh honeycomb, home-made butter, many kinds of cheese, and freshly harvested vegetables.

Some of these markets also sell fresh seafood of all kinds— from cod to Atlantic salmon (if you go to a market near the Atlantic Ocean) or Dover sole in England. Bring a large bag from home and load up on some of the best and freshest food in the country.

"There is no sincerer love than the love of food."

George Bernard Shaw

Carve a Pumpkin

One of the best things to look forward to in the autumn, aside from carving pumpkins and deciding on a costume, is candied apples—it is just not October without them.

Try making your own rather than buying them. Melt down some caramels in a double boiler, put a stick into a good, green granny smith, and dip away. Rest the dipped apples on waxed paper and refrigerate.

"Only the knife knows what goes on in the heart of a pumpkin."

Simone Schwarz-Bart

359

Come On, Get Happy

Your First Day in a New Job!

A new job means new experiences and new people. New responsibilities and a new office or working space is something to be happy about, for sure.

Get in early, the first day is always a frantic one, remembering peoples' names, where they are located, finding out about your new work—it is a new job and a new world.

"Choose a job you love, and you will never have to work a day in your life."

Confucius

Celebrate . . . All Year

Must one just observe Christmas on Christmas Day? We make a point out of creating the classic Christmas dinner—turkey, sweet potatoes, gravy, pumpkin pie, cranberry sauces in December but we can do it in July too. It is fun, it brings family and friends together, once a year is certainly not enough, and it makes us all aware that we do have much to be thankful for—all year round.

Everybody to whom I've mentioned this thought it was a great idea—if everybody pitches in and it doesn't become another reason to keep Mom in the kitchen for two or three days.

"God gave us memories that we might have roses in December."

James M. Barrie

"May We Play Through?"

Take up golf. You don't have to be Tiger Woods; play at your own level and learn to get better. If you really like it, take some lessons. Just being outside is a good enough reason to "pick up the irons."

Find a course that is right for you, there are many public courses as well as private golf and country clubs. Remember, you are out there to have fun and not, necessarily, to hit a hole-in-one.

"If you think it's hard to meet new people, try picking up the wrong golfball."

Jack Lemmon

Let the Flakes Fall Where They May

If you're lucky enough to live in a part of the world where there is a different change in the seasons, then you may love the first snowfall of the winter. It is oddly settling and reconfirms the fact that life goes on, with the promise that holidays and festivals are not far beyond.

The gentle, sometimes almost romantic, quiet falling of the white flakes can help you recall some very pleasant memories—the snowman you built as a child or just catching a few flakes on your tongue, oh, to be a kid again!

"Children are like wet cement. Whatever falls on them makes an impression."

Haim Ginott

Raise a Toast to Yourself!

"I won!"

Whether you have won a new toaster or the Irish Sweepstakes, there is always time for a celebration—I'd rather have the winning ticket for the sweepstakes, but on the other hand, I could use a new toaster . . .

It is great fun to enter contests. Some people I know have won all kinds of things—my friend Julie won a year's supply of burgers, a delicious prize if you ask me.

"This could be you, if you just fill out the simple form . . ."

From a TV ad for Publishers Clearing House

Happiness Is Not Always Loud

Go within yourself for some solitude, there is much happiness to be found in the quietness of just "being." Learn to meditate—or teach yourself your own method of solitude and meditation, you don't need a mantra to find inner peace. There is great happiness in being settled, having a good routine, and living within your own prescribed pace. Happiness is not always external; the kind that lasts comes often from the inside.

Take note: peace and happiness should be synonymous.

"When there is a river in your growing up, you probably always hear it."

Ann Zwinger

365

Come On, Get Happy

Be Strong and Be Happy

In order to be happy, one must live by his or her own convictions, beliefs, and sense of dignity. Take stock of your own and make a mental note of what they are, if you take this inventory you may be surprised, but it will certainly make you happy.

In the face of extreme adversity, we need sometimes to look for additional strength in others, or in a higher power. There is innate goodness, clarity, and ultimately happiness in this exercise.

"Man must search for what is right, and let happiness come on its own."

Johann Pestalozzi

Make
www.thorsonselement.com
your online sanctuary

Get online information, inspiration and
guidance to help you on the path to physical
and spiritual well-being. Drawing on the integrity
and vision of our authors and titles, and with
health advice, articles, astrology, tarot, a
meditation zone, author interviews and events
listings, www.thorsonselement.com is a great
alternative to help create space and peace
in our lives.

So if you've always wondered about practising
yoga, following an allergy-free diet, using the
tarot or getting a life coach, we can point you
in the right direction.

thorsons
element